WALKING *from*
GARSTANG*and*
*in*WYRESDALE

WALKING *from* GARSTANG *and* *in* WYRESDALE

IAN & KRYSIA BRODIE

All internal photographs are copyright of the authors.

First published in 1986, sixth edition 2020
by Palatine Books,
Carnegie House,
Chatsworth Road
Lancaster LA1 4SL
www.carnegiepublishing.com

British Library Cataloguing-in-Publication data
A catalogue record for this book is available from the British Library

ISBN: 978-1-910837-30-6

Designed and typeset by Carnegie Book Production

Printed and bound by Cambrian Printers

Contents

Gilberton, Tarnbrook

Introduction

Welcome to the sixth edition of *Walking from Garstang and in Wyresdale*. The first edition appeared in March 1986 and the book has been in almost continuous production since that date.

This edition contains some of the old favourite walks but feedback from previous editions suggests that some shorter walks more suitable for families should be included. Given our advancing years this was readily adopted for this edition!

The changes mean that whilst we cover a significant proportion of the Wyre Way in some of the walks, the whole route cannot now be followed with this edition. Some 40 km of the most interesting sections of the Wyre Way is covered (around 25 miles of the 41 mile route). The gaps are easily filled in with the Ordnance Survey 1:25000 maps, maps which in any case we advise you to take with you on your walks and which we find add significantly to the enjoyment of the countryside. With the exception of one walk, the two O.S. maps *OL41 Forest of Bowland and Ribblesdale* and *296 Lancaster, Morecambe and Fleetwood* cover the routes. Map *286 Blackpool & Preston* covers the other walk (18) from Brock.

During the life of this edition the new England Coast Path should be opened and we include a couple of walks which cover small sections of this route.

We have taken the opportunity to include greater detail than previous editions of some of the wildlife highlights we often come across on these walks, especially from spring to late summer. We have given more details on some of the dragonflies, butterflies and flowers you could find whilst walking the various routes of the book.

One change from previous editions is that fewer routes are accessible via public transport and this is partly due to some

Abbeystead, Tarnbrook

reductions in services. However, please check our public transport information if you use this means of getting to the start of the walks.

The landscape of the Wyre is greatly contrasting and rarely ever dull. From the upland moors, through the rolling lower fells and down to the coastal plains there is always something of interest, whether in terms of landscape, historical interest or a variety of wildlife. There should be much to interest children in this beautiful area of the English countryside.

It is said that walking books are out of date the day they are published. Stiles can be replaced by kissing gates, paths may become overgrown, for example. Public rights of way are the responsibility of Lancashire County Council but local government cutbacks in expenditure have been unduly heavy on the Council's countryside service. If you do find a problem on the way, please do report it to the Council, perhaps best accessed through their MARIO mapping system which gives you the information you need to make your comments. One planned route had to be omitted from this edition because the paths were physically impossible to use! However, the authors are very grateful for the interest and help of a number of parish councils in ensuring the footpaths used in this book are now in a better condition than we found them.

We have been assisted in compiling this edition by Wyre Borough Countryside Service and the Ramblers (Garstang Group), especially their footpath secretary Bryan Rawlinson. We also offer our thanks to our sometime companions Lesley and Mike Nichols of Garstang.

Enjoy the delights of this fascinating area, please walk responsibly with the Countryside Code in mind, remembering that much of the land over which you walk is someone's workplace.

Ian & Krysia Brodie, September 2019.

A number of the local place names appear to have a Norse origin. Those ending in fell (a hill), dale (valley) being the most obvious. Others include tarn (small lake), beck (stream), clough (or cleugh — a ravine), and Brock (brocc — a badger). Grizedale is the valley of the wild pig (griss). Hazelhurst Fell is the hazel wooded hillside (hyrst). Snape Rake Lane is the track up the hillside (reik).

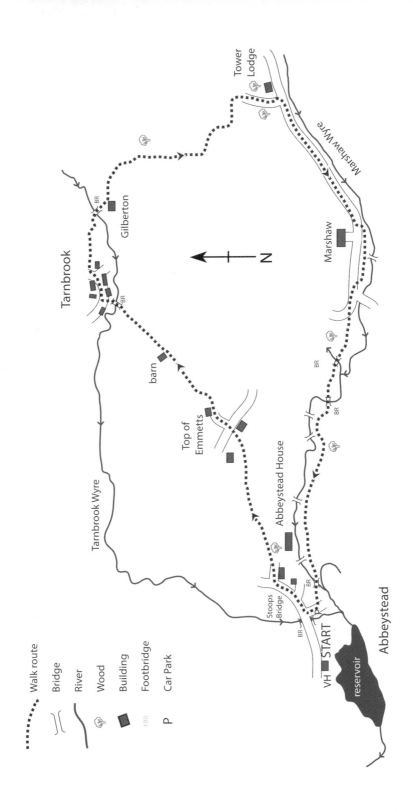

Walk route

Bridge

River

Wood

Building

FBR Footbridge

P Car Park

N

Tarnbrook

Gilberton

BR

Tarnbrook Wyre

barn

Top of Emmetts

Abbeystead House

Stoops Bridge

BR

VH START

reservoir

Abbeystead

Marshaw Wyre

Tower Lodge

Marshaw

BR

BR

The twin rivers

ABBEYSTEAD–TARNBROOK–MARSHAW–ABBEYSTEAD

DISTANCE: 10 kilometres (6 miles)

START: Abbeystead (GR SD563543)

BUS: No service

PARKING: Stoops Bridge, to the east of the village hall by the riverside just east of the bridge (SD563543, LA2 9BQ)

MAP: O.S. Explorer OL41 *The Forest of Bowland & Ribblesdale*

ROUTE: The whole walk forms the upper loop of the Wyre Way

TIP: A pair of binoculars is useful for seeing the local bird life. A good walk on a clear winter day

The River Wyre rises on the fells above Abbeystead and it is formed from two main tributaries, the Marshaw and the Tarnbrook Wyres. This walk explores the dales of these two tributaries. The whole walk (as is most of walk 2) and catchment is on land owned by the Grosvenor Estate of the Duke of Westminster and is managed for shooting and agriculture. The moors were once said to be the most productive red grouse shoot in England whilst the copse-speckled landscape is designed for pheasant and rough shooting. This walk traverses an interesting mixture of landscape types. The moorlands can hold important raptors such as merlin and hen harrier.

Red Grouse

Abbeystead House and its well cared-for gardens are seen from the walk near the end of the route. The area was a medieval hunting chase – a claim that might still ring true today. Also on the route, in various stages of decay, are three privies and, especially around Ouzel Thorn, some good examples of management of landscape features.

From Stoops Bridge, over the Tarnbrook Wyre, walk away from the hamlet past the entrance lodge to Abbeystead House and then climb steeply uphill on the road. When the road bends left leave it to go to the right through the gate adjacent to the cottage and go to enter a field by the kissing gate at the rear of the garage and garden (600 metres).

Follow the right-hand wall and deer fence but when it starts to curve away to the right cross the remainder of the field by going under the overhead power lines and aiming for the farm buildings ahead. Go over the stile by the left of a gate, just to the right of the hare waymark post.

These carved stones on the Wyre Way are a superb contribution by local people to the character of Over Wyresdale parish and often reflect features of the walk.

In this second field follow the left-hand fence to go through the kissing gate by the gate in the far left-hand field corner. Cross the next field to reach the road by a stile found to the left of the right-hand cottage, seen directly ahead (900 metres).

Cross the road, go down the short access track to Top o' Emmetts but just short of the yard turn right, over a stile and follow the left-hand boundary, and then cross the footbridge and stile in the far left-hand corner of the field. In the next field follow the right-hand boundary and, after a short distance, cross the stile to your right, immediately followed by a second stile and plank footbridge (300 metres).

From the stile, views of the amphitheatre of the Tarnbrook Wyre can be seen lying below the slopes of Ward's Stone Fell. To your south is the ridge of Hawthornthwaite Fell.

In the field aim towards the right of a barn whose roof could be seen from the stile. On your way pick up a left-hand fence line by the lapwing stone waymarker, and cross the next stile, footbridge and immediately adjacent stile, in the fence facing you. Go past the right-hand side of the barn and to meet the right-hand fence by the hat stone, then follow the right-hand

Abbeystead House

fence to cross a stone stile in the far right-hand corner. In the next field follow the right-hand wall and fence, cross through the gated gap stile in the field corner, bear slightly left to cross the track and then a further gated gap stile (1km).

Cross the middle of the next field to go over a stile in the short section of stone wall and then directly across the field to climb the stile facing you. Go slightly right and down the next field to cross the stile by the gate at the bottom corner of the field and then cross the gated bridge over the Tarnbrook Wyre. Follow the short, enclosed track to the hamlet of Tarnbrook. Turn right to go through the settlement (380 metres).

The houses of the hamlet are of interest because of their vernacular features. The settlement is a 'closed' village in the Abbeystead estate but at one time it comprised 25 dwellings, of which nine housed Quaker families, and employed the skills of a hundred hatters and glovemakers. Tarnbrook was a vaccary (a farm site, see vaccary information box on page 7).

At the far end of the hamlet go through the gate on the left at the end of the metalled road. Continue along this farm and moorland access track, bear right at the fork to go over the

A Wyre Way marker

cattle grid and through two gates and continue to pass over a second cattle grid just short of Gilberton Farm and the river (750 metres).

Over the cattle grid go left immediately and cross the river by the footbridge upstream from the farm bridge. Continue ahead behind the farm and turn left with a wall on your right. This takes you over a small arched bridge with gate, then over a further bridge, and then a gate to enter a yard between two barns. Bear right in the yard to leave by the first gate between the barns (300 metres).

Turn left in the field and follow the left-hand wall up and then go through the gate in the top left-hand field corner. Continue upwards in the next field going parallel to the left-hand boundary and wood to cross the stile in the top left-hand field corner. Continue up in the third field and go through the prominent gate in the facing boundary (375 metres). Just beyond is a flower marker post.

Continue near the left-hand boundary, ignore the first, wooden, ladder stile but cross the next, iron, ladder stile by the gate. You are now at the highest point of the walk and on the edge of the moor. Here fields can easily revert to moorland vegetation or, with drainage and fertiliser, become grassy fields. Such is the dynamics of the landscape. Go half right to cross the next ladder stile and then half left to cross the stone stepped stile in the wall, an excellent example of 1990s walling (500 metres).

Ahead of you is the view towards the road and the melt-water channel that gives rise to the name Trough of Bowland.

Go diagonally downhill to the far right-hand corner of the field, passing concrete bases of wartime army huts. Part way down there is a stile to enter a newly planted wood which you cross and then continue in the same direction through the wood to reach a stile by a gate. Over this turn right and follow the gated track down to reach the road just beyond the gate at Tower Lodge (375 metres) .

Tower Lodge was intended as a shooting lodge for the never completed Wyresdale Tower on the hill above.

Go right and follow the roadside, with the Marshaw Wyre on your left, until a cattle grid crosses the road (1.5km).

On the left-hand side of the cattle grid go through the kissing gate and follow the right-hand wall down the riverside field.

The upper Tarnbrook Wyre

Cross a small slab footbridge before crossing a further kissing gate. Continue near the right-hand wall to cross a further kissing gate, by a footbridge, and then in the next field, follow the right-hand boundary but, after 30 metres of fence beyond the walled section, cross the kissing gate to gain access to the roadside (500 metres).

Go left on the road, ignore the left turn (to Scorton) and continue until the road bends sharp right. Enter the field directly ahead by the gate and follow the left-hand hedge boundary along until a wall, with a waymark stone, bends away to the left. From here go straight ahead and then down close to the right-hand wood to cross a footbridge, with the river still to your left. Ignore the more obvious footbridge to the left of the wall below you. From here to the start are a number of footbridges across the Marshaw Wyre but many are marked private and are not used on the walk. Pass through the subsequent gate and then follow the path by the left-hand fence until you enter a wider field. Continue ahead to climb the hillock and then descend to a kissing gate and footbridge in the wall facing you. Cross the river here (750 metres).

Go forward in the field to pass a sycamore and then climb gently behind it. Now keep your height above the river, which is down to the right, until the path gets nearer the river when then crosses a relatively level, grassy area. Note the private footbridges. The river then meanders left towards a steep bluff. Opposite the private footbridge turn left up the gap below the steep bluff of the field to find, behind a large fallen oak tree, a flight of stone steps that lead you up the steep embankment and beyond you enter a short section of woodland which you follow along the right-hand fence above the steep riverbank. A stone commemorates a planting, in 1908, of the wood during the ownership of the Lord Sefton. Leave the wood by the kissing gate (400 metres).

Keep near to, but above, the right-hand fence and roughly parallel to the river as you traverse this very long field. You pass the front of Abbeystead House and then gently descend to cross a footbridge near the end of this field (800 metres).

Abbeystead House was built in 1886 by the Earl of Sefton and is Elizabethan in style. The windows have mullions and transoms and it cost £100,000 to build. It is what one wag calls 'a palatial shooting box'.

In the field follow the left-hand fence and then pass through the metal kissing gate by a field gate and cattle-grid before bearing right to reach the metalled road and your start at Stoops Bridge (500 metres).

A VACCARY is a small settlement where cattle were bred and land farmed on the King's behalf in the twelfth and thirteenth centuries. Names of these settlements are still in use today. In upper Wyresdale there were twelve vaccaries and examples met on the walks include Tarnbrook, Catshaw, Emmott, Marshaw and Hawthornthwaite. Others existed in Bleasdale.

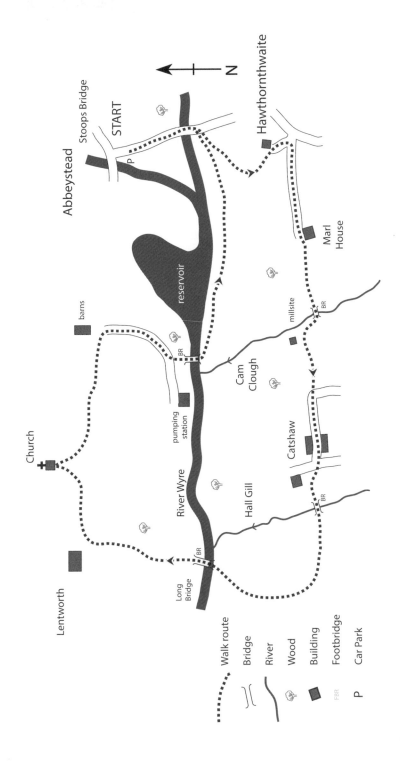

Upper Wyresdale: around Abbeystead

ABBEYSTEAD–CATSHAW–SHEPHERD'S CHURCH–ABBEYSTEAD
RESERVOIR–ABBEYSTEAD

DISTANCE: 6.9 kilometres (4.3 miles)

START: at the car parking area

BUS: No service

PARKING: Stoops Bridge – to the east of the village hall
(SD 564543, LA2 9BQ)

MAP: *O.S. Explorer OL41 The Forest of Bowland & Ribblesdale*

ROUTE: Several paths used in this walk form part of the
variation of the Wyre Way from Abbeystead to Long
Bridge and cover 1 km

TIP: The reservoir can be a good place to see birds so
binoculars could be useful

*An excellent walk downstream of Abbeystead that reflects the
nature of the young River Wyre and provides an ideal complement
to Walk 1 from Abbeystead. Steep wooded bluffs, riverside fields,
and dramatic wooded clough streams tumbling down to the river
are crossed and make this walk of an undulating nature. This
walk passes a number of the interesting locally sculpted waymark
stones which are mostly found on the route of the Wyre Way.
An excellent time to take this walk is during the time of spring*

flowers, particularly during the bluebell flowering of April or
May. For those interested in wildlife the reservoir adds a further
dimension; the architecture of the reservoir spillway provides
another focus of interest. This walk is, however, suitable for most
times of the year. The walk also visits Wyresdale Church, better
known locally as the Shepherd's Church.

Abbeystead is named after the short-lived (perhaps only a
wooden building) Cistercian Abbey that was probably sited at the
confluence of the Marshaw and Tarnbrook Wyres, and built by
monks settling from Furness Abbey. After a short period, during
the twelfth century, the monks moved on to Ireland. Camden
described the scene here as 'solitary and dismal'. You may find
some solitude but the landscape is never dismal.

From Stoops Bridge, over the Tarnbrook Wyre, continue
downstream on the road and cross the next bridge over the
Marshaw Wyre (150 metres). Just below the bridge the two
upper Wyre streams combine to carry their waters from the
Bowland Fells down to Morecambe Bay.

Immediately over the bridge drop down right to follow the left
of two paths through the woods. Some 10 metres after the small
footbridge go left on the right of way, ignoring a permissive
path that carries straight on, and climb the wooded bluff up a
series of steps. On top bear right to cross a stile by a gate and
enter a field (250 metres).

Go left in the field and follow the left-hand fence along the wood
and depression and cross the stile between two gates. Cross
the next field to go through the gateway in the far left-hand
corner and then along the right-hand fence to Hawthornthwaite
Farm. The right of way passes, through two small gates, to the
immediate right of the farmhouse. Past the house, go right on
the track, go through a gate with a stile, and soon bend left to go
along a sunken lane towards the modern farm buildings. Go over
the stile by the gate and then immediately to the right of the

nearside of these buildings and follow the track along to reach Marl House Farm (1km).

From this track are extensive views of the amphitheatre of the upper Wyre catchment.

Continue along the track to the pass the front of the farmhouse, pass through the gate facing you and then cross the stile by the next gate also facing you. In the next field follow parallel to the left-hand fence and then descend to a gated footbridge over the interesting beck in Cam Clough (400 metres).

The rocks of the bed of Cam Clough show the wonderful carving action of the down rushing stream although fallen trees now obscure some of the interest. The smoothness, texture and shape of the bedrock are worth pausing to see.

Cam Clough

Climb the steps ahead, then follow the fenced embankment to the right and, towards its end, bear left to cross a track and gently climb the path in the woods above some ruined buildings to your right. Cross the stile in the fence ahead, cross the narrow field directly ahead to go down to cross a footbridge and then climb some stone steps and a stile (300 metres).

A Wyre Way marker

The embankment was of a reservoir that served the buildings, the remains of an old cotton mill built in 1784, with waterpower. The mill burned down the mid-nineteenth century. Some cottage walls also remain. The remote mill never had a settlement of any size associated with it and the remoteness is a reflection on the vital need for water power.

In the next field follow the left-hand fence and continue in the same direction along the farm track to arrive, through a gate, into the yard of Little Catshaw Farm (1763). On your way a carved waymark stone (a ram's head) is passed. Through the yard follow the farm road and, at the junction cross directly to a stile on the right of a wooden structure (800 metres).

A shorter way to Long Bridge goes right into the yard of Catshaw Hall Farm (1678). The hall was an ancient manorial residence and, like Hawthornthwaite, was listed in 1324 as a vaccary (cattle farm – see text box on p. 7). The building has charm and vernacular interest and still contains some ancient woodwork including a black oak staircase thought to be as old as the house. This path is shown on the O.S. map.

In the field go to pass the left-hand edge of the farm structures, and then follow the left-hand fence steeply down the field to find a stile. Cross this stile and the next one immediately to your right. Follow the gently sloping path down to cross a footbridge (300 metres). The wooden footbridge was built over a sadly derelict packhorse bridge over Hall Gill. Climb to the right up the gently rising path through the wood to arrive at a kissing gate. In the next field go up the slope, pass the obvious rock, and continue in this direction until a small conifer wood can be seen ahead. Aim for this, but before you reach the fence across your way you can note a wooden post with waymark arrows. Turn right here and go down the field, moving gradually closer to the left-hand fence of the wood, to the bottom field corner where a kissing gate admits you into Mark Holme Wood. Follow the path steeply down through the wood to arrive at Long Bridge over the River Wyre. Your way lies over the bridge (600 metres). As you walk up through this last field extensive views open up to Hawthornthwaite Fell on your left and later to the Abbeystead fells on your right.

Whilst by the Wyre look for the white bib of the dipper or watch it perched, bobbing on a river side boulder. Wagtails or the flashing blue iridescence of the kingfisher may be seen. For a shorter walk, but omitting the church, follow the Wyre Way to the right along the bank of the river to reach the reservoir (see the path on your O.S. Map).

Christ Church, Abbeystead, also known as the Shepherd's Church

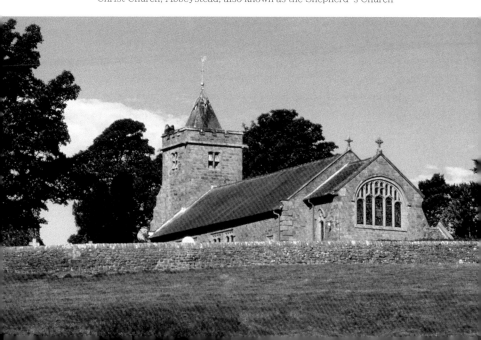

Stained glass windows in the Shepherd's Church

To reach the church go directly ahead from the footbridge, cross the narrow field to go over a stile, climb a few steps through the narrow wood, and then climb the top stile. Go straight ahead to cross the track and follow, near the right-hand fence, to climb steeply up the field. This next section is on a permissive route avoiding the farmyard. Climb the stile, to the right of two adjacent gates found just to the left of the top right-hand corner of the field. Follow along the left-hand fence and farm buildings until you are level with Lentworth House Farm. Continue directly ahead to reach, across the open field, a stone wall (500 metres). Should you wish to follow the right of way, this goes through the left-hand of the two gates by the stile and directly ahead through the farmyard until you are at a kissing gate facing the farmstead. Turn right through this gate.

Turn right and follow the short left-hand wall, noting the weather vane with the waymark stone (a duck) below it just to your left. After the wall bends away left continue directly ahead, heading for the distant grey barns, until the field dips down via a

carved stone (a bird), to where you cross two consecutive stiles
and a footbridge. Climb the field to enter Wyresdale churchyard
by a gate and waymark stone (a bird of prey) (550 metres).

*Christ Church is the Shepherd's Church. It sits high above the Wyre
with its gargoyle waterspouts leaning out from the squat tower of
local stone. The church site dates back to at least the fourteenth
century. The church was rebuilt in 1733, but when the estate
passed to the Sefton family, it was extended. The pulpit dates from
1684. The church is usually open but telephone the vicar (01524
792327) in advance of your visit to be sure of admission. Inside the
church porch you can see wooden bars with iron hooks used by the
shepherds to hang their crooks and lanterns. The windows date
from the turn of the century and represent biblical pastoral scenes
but set in the local landscape. All feature sheep. There was once
on display a 'Geneva' bible printed in 1599, being so named after
the place where the bible was translated into English during times
of persecution under Mary Tudor in this country. It is called the
'breeches bible' due to the modesty of the translators, as we read
in Genesis 3 verse 7 that Adam and Eve made themselves breeches.*

Above Abbeystead

Abbeystead reservoir spillway

Just above the church and vicarage is the Sunday School housed above the original public stable. The original 1733 vicarage lies further to the north.

Return to the gate by which you entered the churchyard and go half left down the field aiming for the central group of farm buildings to reach, in the bottom far corner of the field, a stile which you cross and then a footbridge. Climb up from the stream and again aiming for the grey barns to cross a stile by a gate. Then aim half-right to reach a stile in the right-hand edge of space between the buildings. Go down the concrete road to your right, go through the gate by the cattle-grid and then follow the lower track down by the wall (with a rabbit waymark stone) and pass through a double gate to the reservoir dam enclosure (600 metres).

Continue down the obvious track ahead, keep to the left after a small building and follow, above the riverbank, down towards a wall. Turn left over the elaborate footbridge (200 metres).

The area around the dam to Abbeystead Reservoir has a rebuilt fish pass ladder, a grotto-like draw well and the superb spillway where overflowing waters make a delightful sound. The reservoir has largely infilled with sediment and forms a haven for bird-life. Downstream of the footbridge can be seen stone structures that are part of the water supplies – water is piped to here from the River Lune. This is the scene of the 1984 tragedy when a methane explosion killed a number of visitors and staff. The reservoir was built originally for a supply to Lancaster in the early nineteenth century but is now owned by the estate and access to the dam structures is now forbidden.

Over the footbridge, turn left and follow the distinct (permissive) path that follows the reservoir and, later, the river edge to return you to the road where you started the walk (1km).

The name BOWLAND, or more correctly pronounced as BOLLAND, translates as the land of the cattle, and is a reference to the urus, the wild cattle present in the wilder parts of Britain in pre-Roman days.

Lentworth House Farm, Abbeystead

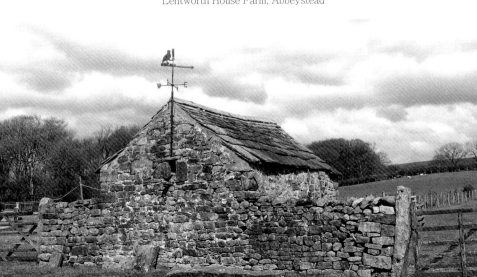

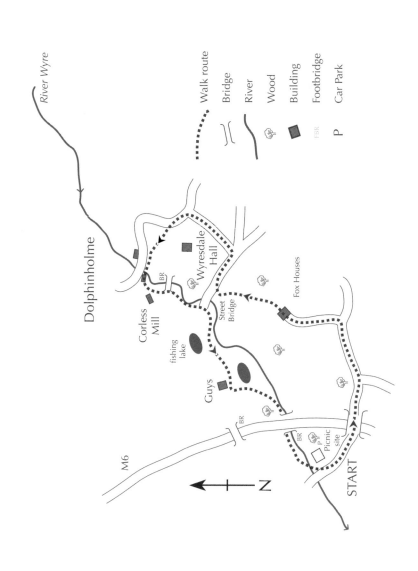

River Wyre

Walk route

Bridge

River

Wood

Building

FBR

P Car Park

Footbridge

Dolphinholme

Wyresdale Hall

Corless Mill

BR

Fox Houses

Street Bridge

fishing lake

Guys

M6

BR

BR

Picnic site

P

START

N

Nether Wyresdale and Dolphinholme

SCORTON–DOLPHINHOLME–SCORTON

DISTANCE: 8 kilometres (5 miles)

START: Scorton Picnic Site, a mile north of the village centre (SD504504)

BUS: None direct to start. The Preston–Lancaster service 40 stops at Casanova's, Hollins Lane, Forton (previously The New Holly), some 2km from the picnic site but walking in the road is not readily advised. Alternatively you can walk from Scorton on the Wyre Way – this adds 3 km in total to the route

PARKING: Scorton Picnic Site on Cleveley Bank Lane at the start of the walk (PR3 1BU)

MAP: O.S. Explorer OL41 *The Forest of Bowland & Ribblesdale*

ROUTE: Some 4 km of the Wyre Way is covered

TIP: An interesting route at its best in spring

This walk explores the middle reach of the River Wyre with some interesting woodlands, noted for flowers in spring, and passes near some extensive water bodies which are the result of previous sand and gravel extraction. A number of interesting buildings can be seen from the route. Some quiet roads are used but some of these have interesting verges especially for spring flowers.

Leave Scorton picnic site, turn left on the road, cross over the M6 and then turn left at the road junction. Continue down this lane, pass the thatched cottage, and when the road begins to bend to the right turn left down a public footpath also marked as a private road. Follow this to the properties at Foxhouses at the end of this road (1km).

Go directly ahead between the houses to find an enclosed path which soon leads to a stile and entry into a field. Follow along the right-hand field boundary and then pass through the kissing gate in the far right-hand field corner. In the next field go along the left-hand boundary, above the stream (Lordhouse Brook) and then climb the stile by an old gate in the far corner of the field. Bear left in the wood, go down over the footbridge and continue to follow this meandering path passing a pond to reach a track. Go right on the track and when it bends right, just before a bridge, turn left on the path that continues through the wood. This path eventually leads to a stile and into the field (650 metres).

In the field follow along the right-hand fence (passing an old hedge line on your left) and continue to cross a stile in the far corner of the field. Some of the woodland has only been present since the cessation of the sand and gravel working, and the

Broad-bodied chaser

large lake seen from this last field is also the result of that former industry. Over the stile continue by the left-hand fence but when a gate is seen to your right cross the small, private area with its seat and hut, and use the path to the

Blackthorn sloes

left of the gate to reach the road beyond (350 metres).

If you want a shorter walk our return route can be found immediately to the left, over Street Bridge.

Turn right on the road and go left up Wagon Road towards Dolphinholme. Views of Harrisend and Hawthornthwaite fells open up to your right. Keep left at the junction with Tinkers Lane, pass the rear entry to Wyreside Hall on your left and, after a short climb, cross the footbridge and stile on your left opposite the track to Wyreside Cottage. Cross the narrow field bearing half-right to a stile over which you follow an enclosed and partly wooded path to a further stile. Over the stile aim for the buildings seen to the right of the gate to cross a further stile. Extensive views of Clougha and Ward's Stone, the fells above Wyresdale, appear from this path. In this large field bear half-left, through the line of oak trees and gradually come closer to the left-hand field boundary and wood. At the lowest point to this field side, near a ruined chimney, is a stile that leads you down through a shorter section of wood to the road. Go left down to Dolphinholme Bridge (1km).

On the building on the left before the bridge is a restored old gas lamp and reflects the fact that Dolphinholme Mill, a worsted mill of 1787, was one of the first in the country to be illuminated by gas lights (1801). The ruined chimney you have passed was from the flue of the gas works, which was sited in what is now the garden of the first property on your left. The mill, originally and unusually spinning worsted rather than cotton, employed a thousand spinners, whilst wool was combed in houses. The mill warehouse (1797), just over the bridge, is now a terrace of houses. From here back to Scorton you follow the Wyre Way. The name Dolphinholme may have originated as Tolfinsholme, after a Norseman who may have settled on an island (holme) in the river. For further details of all the water-powered mills passed on your walks in this book consult Chris Aspin's book The Water-Spinners: A new look at the early cotton trade.

Cross the bridge and just above the mill houses, turn left off the road and take the lower of two paths to pass the sewage treatment plant and continue along a path with the wood on your right and, shortly, a wall on your left. Follow this path for its full length, pass through the small gate across your way and then cross the field aiming for the left-hand side of the farmhouse. Go into the yard by the small gate adjacent to the left-hand side of the house with the water wheel of Corless Mill also on your left (800 metres).

This former corn and wool weaving mill still displays the reconstructed seventeen-foot diameter and five-foot wide waterwheel, two millstones and, at Keepers Cottage, a curious-shaped roof. When wool was woven it is said that children were

Corless Mill, Dolphinholme

Corless Mill water wheel, Dolphinholme

brought from Liverpool as cheap labour and it was reputed to be a most unhappy place.

Go along the mill access track, pass Keepers Cottage and climb up the track with the river down to your left. As the track climbs and bends to the right go through a small gateway on your left. This leads you along a path above the river, through a small wood, and then by a footbridge into the field. Follow the riverbank path down, through two small gates either side of the drive and bridge to Wyreside Hall, and continue along the riverbank to reach the road by steps and a gate (550 metres).

Wyreside Hall, dated 1852, with its dark grey stone, giant pilaster and porch of fluted Ionic columns, is well sited to enjoy views of the river valley. If you took the short cut over Street Bridge, rejoin our route here.

From the facing steps and gate the path continues above the riverbank through a wood and eventually leads you, via a gate, onto a track at the end of a fishing lake. Wyreside Fishery is part of the Duchy of Lancaster Estate activities. Go left on the track and follow it along as it bends right and goes through a further gate to reach the car park on the nearside of the house, Sunnyside. This is a major tourism area and many caravans have

Wyreside Hall seen from the path

to be passed on this section of the walk. At the garden wall turn left to pass through the gate by the children's playground (to your left) and go directly ahead on the caravan access track to reach a wooden hut. Go to the right of this through a small gate and then turn left in the field. Follow the left-hand ditch along until the hedgerow crosses to your side of the ditch bank. From here cross the remainder of the field towards the left-hand side of the buildings ahead where there is a small gate you cross situated half-way along the field boundary facing you. This is the former Guy's Farm and is a Girl Guide camp. Go directly ahead and pass down the left-hand side of these buildings, under the archway and, at the end of the buildings, turn right onto the track that passes the front of the house (1.2km).

The Wyre Way from here to your starting point is not as shown on maps due to recent changes in the footpath network. From the track in front of Guy's Farm turn left and follow the track along until signs divert you to the right near a large lake. The route now follows above the River Wyre, under the M6 by the riverbank, and continues by the edge of the field along until the

Kingfisher

Grasshopper warbler

path through the wood becomes a distinct path (with the river still on your left). On reaching the road turn left over Cleveley Bridge to return to your starting point.

THE FOREST OF BOWLAND was thus named as it was covered by laws applying to its status as a Royal Forest. These game preserves were set up largely after the Norman Conquest. The Forest Law could be harsh on local residents, especially if they had been poaching. This part of Lancashire had a number of hunting forests. The upper reaches of the Wyre were, for example, part of the Royal Forest of Wyresdale. The area is a designated an Area of Outstanding Natural Beauty although some would claim it is deserving of National Park status.

Wyreside by Street Bridge

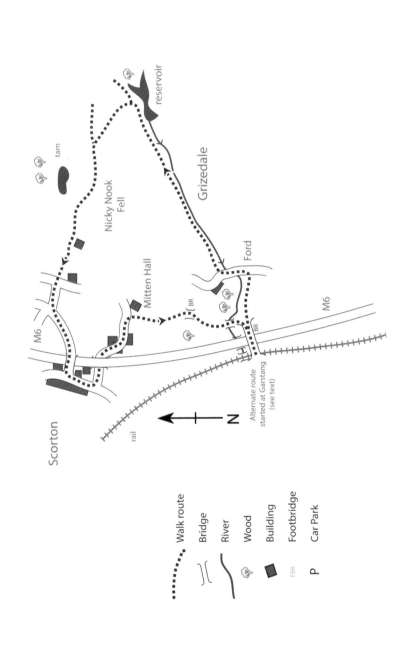

Scorton

rail

M6

Nicky Nook
Fell

tarn

reservoir

Mitten Hall

Grizedale

Ford

BR

BR

M6

Alternate route
started at Garstang
(see text)

N

Walk route

Bridge

River

Wood

Building

FBR Footbridge

P Car Park

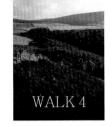
Nicky Nook: a perennial favourite

SCORTON–GRIZEDALE–NICKY NOOK–SCORTON

DISTANCE: 8 kilometres (5 miles). A longer, alternative route starting from Garstang of 11.5 km (7 miles) can also be undertaken

START: Scorton village (SD502488). The walk can also be started from the Garstang High Street car park (see walk 5)

BUS: Scorton is served only by school buses. Garstang is served by regular services from Lancaster, Preston and Blackpool (Services 40, 41, and 42)

PARKING: Roadside parking, with care, can be found in Scorton village (PR3 1AU). A pay and display at Garstang's High Street car park is appropriate for the longer route

MAP: O.S. Explorer OL41 The Forest of Bowland & Ribblesdale

ROUTE: 4 km of the Wyre Way from Scorton to Garstang are covered in the longer route

TIP: We enjoy this walk most in bluebell flowering time, although it is a walk for all seasons

This is the classic route for walkers from Garstang despite the need to use sections of country lanes. However a shorter, more family friendly walk is featured staring at Scorton but details of

Grizedale

the longer walk are added. The walk encompasses the local fells, woodlands and water – elements which combine to make the Lancashire countryside so attractive. Refreshments and toilets are available in Scorton and Garstang. Scorton is an attractive village with the older properties built of the local gritstone but it is often extremely busy with tourists. The 'Score' of Scorton is probably a small narrow ravine-shaped dell just above the village. As there was water power there was an Arkwright machinery cotton mill in the area.

From the Square start up Snowhill Lane but soon turn right in front of the war memorial and pass the school as you walk down the driveway to the church. Go through the lychgate into the church grounds. The building of 1878–9 is a typical solid stone design of Paley and Austin reflecting Victorian values, and cost £14,000 to build. Just beyond the tower turn right on the tarred path to go through a small gate and then descend the field, past a huge oak tree, to a further gate and the road (270 metres).

Turn left on the road and, just after the bowling club, left again into Tithebarn Lane. Go under the M6 and continue on the road

to pass a group of houses on the left-hand bend. After the last house on the right, East Barn, go up the road to find a kissing gate in the hedge above the top of the garden. The footpath sign points us towards Garstang and informs us we are on the route of the Wyre Way (550 metres).

In the field cross parallel to the M6 and pick up the left-hand fence that passes the house, Mitten Hall, and leads towards a gateway in the far left-hand field corner with a small gate to the right of this gate. In the next field aim for the metal gate to the left of the corner of the replanted wood ahead. Continue along the right-hand fence of the wood to a wooden footbridge and kissing gate that allows you to enter the wood. Turn left to go through the older section of wood and follow the track through the wood to a gate (with a stile on its left) (900 metres).

This wood is at its best during the bluebell flowering time in spring.

Through this gate cross the field towards the right-hand corner and the side of the M6 to go over a footbridge. Zigzag left then right up the embankment to climb to a track with the M6 just off to your right (300 metres).

Grizedale Reservoir from Nicky Nook

The longer route from and to Garstang joins and leaves our route here. To return to Garstang go right on the track and recross the motorway and railway bridges to pick up the description in the Garstang to Scorton Walk (number 5).

Follow the track to the left along to a stile and gate and continue beyond on this track with the wood on your left. Continue down to a stile and gate and the metalled lane beyond. Go left down the lane that crosses two streams, past the entrance to Throstle Nest houses on your left, and shortly, as the road starts to climb, a track signed as a bridle path to Nicky Nook goes off to your right (1.1km).

Walkers up Nicky Nook

Go along this track, through the gate and along the beck-side path until, just after a footbridge to your right, you go through the facing gate, by a stile, to continue along the obvious track as it climbs up the dale to arrive, after a further gate and kissing-gate, at Grizedale reservoir (1.7km).

Grizedale was dammed in 1861–3. Whilst the waters are too acidic to be able to support much life it is not without its interests. Grizedale is Norse for the valley of the wild pigs. The valley contains many birch and oak trees and gives an indication of what the whole valley might have been like in more ancient times. The narrow valley, Nicky Nook is certainly a Nook and perhaps, given

the late afternoon arrival of the sun into the valley floor, it may
have been anciently perceived as the home of Old Nick (the devil)!

Continue along the track until almost opposite the fork in the reservoir there is a break in the left-hand fence that gives access to stone steps and a stile in the wall with a footpath sign to Scorton and Nicky Nook. Cross the stile and climb the steep path, later with steps, that keeps near the right-hand fence and wall until, on the more gentle slope, the obvious path bears to your left and climbs gently to the triangulation point on the fell top at a height of 215 metres (850 metres).

The fell offers extensive views of the Forest of Bowland moors,
the Lakeland fells, the Fylde Plain and Morecambe Bay. On clear
days the Isle of Man and North Wales can be seen. The spread of
rhododendron and the state of some of the walls on parts of the
fell and in Grizedale cry out for urgent attention.

Leave the top by continuing along in the same direction as previously and as if heading towards Morecambe Bay. The path leads towards a broke-wall corner and then down and curves right towards the trees above the topmost tarn. Keep to the left of these trees and follow an obvious path, later with steps, which lead down to a kissing gate above a small reservoir and then more steeply down to a kissing gate to emerge by a road junction. Follow the road directly across that leads all the way down to Scorton village (2km).

Speckled wood butterfly

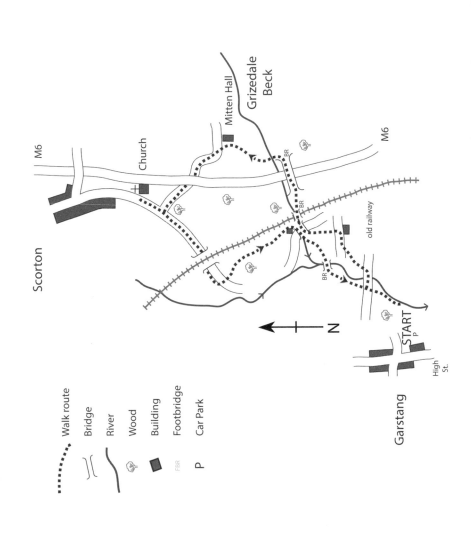

Walk route

Bridge

River

Wood

Building

Footbridge

Car Park

Scorton

M6

Church

Mitten Hall

Grizedale Beck

M6

old railway

BR

BR

BR

N

START

High St.

Garstang

Garstang to Scorton

GARSTANG–SCORTON–GARSTANG

DISTANCE: 8 km (5 miles)

START: Garstang High Street car park

BUS: Garstang is served by regular services from Lancaster, Preston and Blackpool (Services 40, 41, X42, and 42)

PARKING: A pay and display at Garstang High Street. (SD493454, PR3 1FA)

MAP: *O.S. Explorer OL41 The Forest of Bowland & Ribblesdale*

ROUTE: 4 km of the Wyre Way, from Scorton to Garstang, are covered

TIP: Avoid this route if there has been very heavy rain

This walk provides a pleasant circular route between the two settlements and the route can be used to link with Walk 4, the Nicky Nook walk, and turn that into a 12.5 Km (8 mile) longer excursion. Garstang is referred to as 'Cherestanc' in the Doomsday Book and had several coaching inns for the London to Edinburgh route. A Thursday market has been held since 1310.

From the rear of High Street riverside car park go to the riverbank, turn left and follow the path along the sports field-edge path and riverbank towards the bridge, and then climb the steps up the near side of the bridge abutment (400 metres).

The bridge crosses the extraction point from the Lune–Wyre Conjunctive Use Scheme; from here water supplies are piped to the Franklaw Treatment Works at Catterall before joining the North West supply grid. The upstream barriers are to prevent flood-waters from inundating villages down stream through flooding the surrounding fields. This walk is therefore not useable at times of flood.

Go right, over the bridge, and just after the embankment track has joined from the left go left down steps, through a kissing gate, and then across the field to a further gate. In the next field continue in the same direction to pass through a further gate near the right-hand field corner. Go across the next field to meet the left-hand boundary, which is followed to a further kissing gate, by a field-gate, and gives you access to access to Lingart Lane (500 metres).

Go right along the lane, and immediately over the small-stream bridge and when opposite the track to the farm, go over the stile on your left. Cross the middle of the field to cross the footbridge in the facing hedge. Follow the right-hand fence (this was decrepit in 2019 and may be changed) in the next field, go over the stile in the far right-hand corner and continue along the fence line and, when it bends away to your right, continue straight ahead to reach the bank of Grizedale Brook (500 metres).

Bear right here near the stream but then go directly to pass through the gate in the section of stone wall at the far end of the field on an obvious path. Cross the road diagonally right

Garstang High Street

Grizedale

and go down the short track to the left of the industrial buildings to reach the railway (750 metres). Some of this path does not strictly coincide with the public right of way but is more easily walkable.

Cross the railway footbridge and subsequent motorway bridge (200 metres).

This, for walkers going to Nicky Nook, is where you pick up the route description from Scorton to take you over Nicky Nook in Walk 4.

Over the motorway go slightly left to zig-zag down the bank (though the gorse bushes) and cross the obvious footbridge. From here walk ahead, with the motorway to your left, to an obvious gate and stile which lead into the wood. This is Woodacre Great Wood and a perfect place to observe bluebells in spring. Follow the obvious path through the wood and when you arrive at the newly planted section go right, through the kissing gate and over the footbridge into the field (500 metres).

Go left along the wood edge, pass through the small gate in the left-hand field corner and cross the next field to a further small gate seen between the left-hand two (of three) single oak trees directly ahead. Follow the right-hand boundary along, pass the house and then cross the remainder of the field to an obvious metal kissing gate which gives you access to Tithe Barn Lane (450 metres).

Go left down the lane to meet the main road through Scorton by the bowling green (650 metres).

The facilities of the attractive Scorton Village can be found to your right. The village is often busy especially at weekends with visitors. Your route to return to Garstang starts from this road junction.

Return route

Turn away from the village at the bowling club and go under the arch of the railway bridge. Continue along the pavement by the River Wyre, up the ramp and, after three seats, go down the access track by the mosaic of a snail to the road. Turn right and cross the road and, just after the last dwelling, go through the kissing gate on your left (450 metres).

In the field follow the left-hand fence along to cross a stile by a gate by the large outbuildings and then go ahead towards the

Near Woodacre

Peacock butterfly

Painted lady butterfly

next gate. Turn right to pass through a series of gates and a stile until you come to the edge of the house on your right. Go directly ahead to a stile and gate to enter a field. Follow the left-hand boundary until a stone gap stile and wooden stile are found on your left. Cross this into the next field (400 metres).

Follow to the right of the fence and continue until you reach a gate in the far left-hand corner of the field, just before your reach Horse Coppy Wood. Go left through the gate, turn immediately right to cross a very small stream and go through the gate and stile by the wood corner. Contour above the wood on your right to go towards some small stone-built housing. Before this is reached cross the stile on your right, follow the left-hand boundary to cross a further stile and the road. Go left on the road, pass over Grizedale Brook, and re-reach the gate you used on your route out from Garstang (900 metres).

Go down the field on the obvious path, soon with the brook on your right, and follow this all the way down to its confluence with the River Wyre. Turn left, go through the small gate, and climb the slight rise of Broom Hill, a much-eroded small glacial drumlin, and then descend to a further small gate and regain the riverbank path. Go along to pass the aqueduct and then go over the subsequent Lingart footbridge and to reach Wyre Lane (1km).

Cross the lane to a small gate, to enter Garstang Millennium Green, and follow the path along to a further gate by a wooden sculpture of a dipper. The surfaced path follows the riverbank via a stepped embankment and enables you to return easily to your starting point in Garstang (1km).

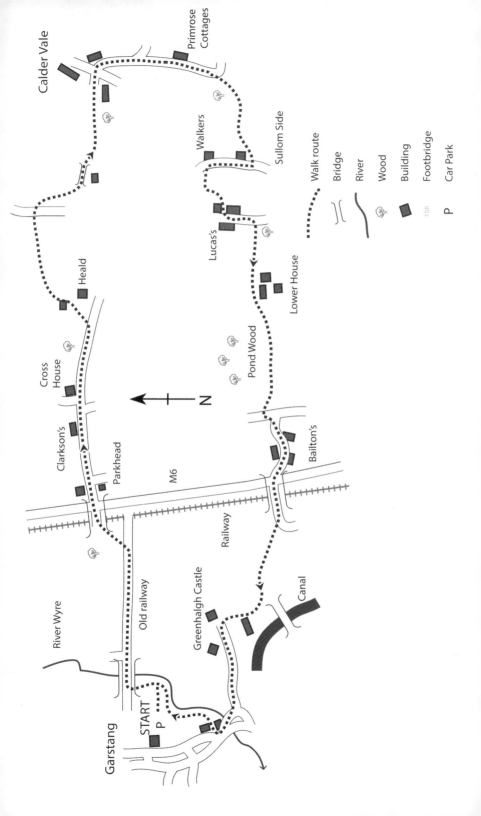

Calder Vale

Primrose Cottages

Walkers

Sullom Side

Heald

Cross House

Clarkson's

Parkhead

M6

Lucas's

Lower House

Pond Wood

Bailton's

Railway

Greenhalgh Castle

Canal

River Wyre

Old railway

Garstang

START
P

Walk route

Bridge

River

Wood

Building

FBR   Footbridge

P   Car Park

N

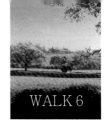

Mills on the Calder

GARSTANG–CALDER VALE–GARSTANG

DISTANCE: 8.5 kilometres (5.5 miles)

START: Garstang car park at north end of High Street
(GR 493454)

BUS: Garstang lies on the main Preston to Lancaster route
(services 40, 41) and Lancaster to Blackpool route
(service 42)

PARKING: Park in Garstang High Street car park. (GR SD493454,
PR3 1FA)

MAP: O.S. Explorer OL41 *The Forest of Bowland & Ribblesdale*

ROUTE: Only 900 metres of the Wyre Way, through Garstang

TIP: Another walk we enjoy most during the bluebell
flowering season (around April–May)

*A walk mostly over field paths and tracks that combines aspects
of industrial archaeology with fine prospects of the landscape. In
bluebell time the woods along the route can be spectacular but
this walk is an all year round favourite because of the views across
the Fylde plain to the coast, to Morecambe Bay and towards the
moorlands of the Forest of Bowland.*

**From the north end of the High Street go right, across the car
park, to the river and follow the path upstream (the sports field
is on your left) to reach the embankment and bridge across the**

Above Heald Farm to Bowland

River Wyre. Go up the steps on the left near side and then go over the bridge and continue directly ahead through the small gateway facing you beyond the end of the tarmac track (400m).

The bridge was formerly the site of the crossing point of the old Garstang to Knott End railway known locally as the 'Pilling Pig'. It operated, largely unsuccessfully, between 1870 and 1963.

Continue along the enclosed path, the former route of the railway, down over a small stream, up to pass through a small gate and continue directly ahead under the overhead power lines. Just beyond here, and just short of where the trackbed enters a cutting, follow up the left-hand embankment to a stile by a memorial seat and above a set of steps (800m).

The cutting took the railway to join the mainline near the former Garstang and Catterall Station but now, from the bottom of the steps, it forms a memorial nature reserve to which you have permissive access. In the cutting are smaller exposures of the underlying friable sandstone, a rock that serves as an aquifer.

Over the stile go half-right across the field, pass the corner of the wood aiming for the motorway bridge and pass through the gap by the metal gate in the far corner of the field. Turn right

on the track to cross over the railway and the motorway, with a stream crossing on the bridge, to reach Parkhead (500m).

Go straight ahead and up the gated metalled access track, ignoring any paths or turns off to the right or left and eventually go to pass Clarkson's Farm, on your left, and continue up to meet the road where it bends. Your way is directly across to the right of white painted Cross House and cottage and up the track towards Heald Farm (550m).

The houses are named after the site of a wailing cross, whose base stone is apparently now buried, where coffin bearers could rest and the mourners wail.

The concrete track climbs past a wood on your left and, just short of the buildings of Heald Farm, turn left over a stile into the bottom of the next, smaller wood. Go up the wood, near the left-hand fence, and leave it by the stile and gate in the top corner. Go left along the short track to cross a stile by a gate and then go ahead into the field by another gateway by a ruined ladder stile. Turn right and follow the right-hand boundary up to the top of the field (600m).

This is the highest point of the walk and from where extensive views across the Fylde to the coast, Morecambe Bay and the Lake District can be enjoyed. Eastward lies the moors of the Forest of Bowland AONB.

Cross the stile in the top right-hand field corner and go downhill by the right-hand boundary over a further stile (a new wood now lies to the left and, on the right, part of the boundary is a line of beech trees), and leave the wood by a small gate in the corner. Continue by the right-hand boundary, go through a small

Emperor dragonfly ovipositing

gate by a field gate and, almost immediate, join the road by a stile by the gate. The horse training area is an obvious feature along with an incongruous wind turbine. Turn right and cross the road diagonally towards the gateway to 'The Paddocks' and, in front of the gate, go right along a short enclosed path and cross the stile at the end. Continue on an enclosed path by the right-hand ditch and cross a further stile, bear left and again follow the short enclosed path to cross a footbridge and enter a field. Cross the field by aiming for the stone cottage to find a stile in the fence across your way and, over this stile, go to cross field towards an obvious stile at the left-hand corner of the wood (750m).

Over this stile follow an enclosed path that leads along the left-hand edge of the wood, passes the rear gardens of houses and down some steps to the road into Calder Vale (200m).

The centre of the village and the last working mill are down to the left. Calder Vale is a most unexpected place – an industrial stone-built village enveloped in the fold of the Bowland hills. The vernacular architecture is not without character. Lappet Mill was built as a four-storey cotton mill in 1835 with thick stone outer walls and cast-iron pillars. There are remains of the former mill-

Calder Vale

race and mill-pond above the village. The waterwheel was replaced by a turbine, later a beam engine and, in 1909, a gas engine, but is now electrically driven. The mill and village were built for the Jacksons, a Quaker family. The lack of a public house in the village is due to the family not wishing to see 'ragged children'. Brothers Richard and Jonathan founded the cotton mill whilst brother John opened a paper mill upstream at Oakenclough. The mill still operates and its products includes head scarfs for the Arabian markets. Each May the village organises Sunday bluebell walks (free) and tea in the village hall.

From where you emerged on the road turn right down Albert Terrace and follow along the track to the isolated terrace of Primrose Cottages (500m).

The track passes through steep-sided woodlands that are, each spring, carpeted in bluebells, passes above the lodge of the other village mill and the rocky-bed of the River Calder to reach the terrace formerly comprising twelve mill workers' cottages and mill-owners' house. The Barnace Weaving Mill has been demolished but reservoir sites and a mill-race can be seen from the walk. This mill, sited beyond the cottages, opened in 1845 and was powered by a waterwheel and, later, a steam engine whose chimney was constructed up the hillside.

Continue past the cottages and gate until the track bends sharply left to a private business. Go right and climb the sloping path up through the wood to re-enter a field by a gate. Follow the left-hand fence to pass through a further gate in the far left-hand field corner. Continue along the left-hand fence and the subsequent track downhill and, by two further gates, to reach the road by Sullom Side Farm (900m).

Follow the road to the right to reach the next building, Walker House. Cross the road to a gate and stile and re-enter a field. Go down the first field by the right-hand boundary, pass through a gate, and go diagonally left to aim for the farm-house and

enter the rear of Lucas's Farm by a gate and stile (550m).

Greenhalgh Castle

Go down by the right-hand side of the house, turn left on the farm access road and, after thirty metres, go through a small kissing gate on your right just prior to a small wood. Go down the wood edge, over a further stile and then directly down the longer field to a footbridge and stile by a gate in the far bottom left-hand corner (hidden beyond the outbuildings of Lower House) (250m).

Over the stile turn right and go to a stile in the lower right-hand corner of the field that lies opposite a pond in Janet's Hill Wood. The wood has a eucalyptus tree planted in the 1990s as a memorial to a soldier who died in Burma in 1945. However, the tree is being outcompeted. Continue along the right-hand boundary to the corner of the wood (the tree is just to your right), cross the stile (by the memorial stone to the Rostrons who farmed here for 35 years) and go left across the field to cross a further stile by an obvious gate some 20 metres from the left-hand field corner (150m).

Cross the road diagonally left and go down the access track to buildings of Bailton's Farm. The right of way goes through the gated, cobbled yard and then bends right to cross the bridges over both the motorway and the railway line (500m). It is possible that a bypass route to the right of the farm buildings can be taken.

Over the railway bridge go down the track, through a gate, and when the track bends left go through the metal gate ahead. **Cross the next field aiming for the distant church tower, with mini-spire, to reach the right of a lone oak tree standing proud of the far boundary where you cross a further stile. Go directly cross the next short field, aiming left of the pylon, to pass through a gate over a dyke, and then follow the left-hand boundary to the field corner where you cross the stile and plank footbridge facing you (450m).**

[If you want to return to Garstang by the canal towpath you can access it by going through the gate to the left of this stile and walking a short distance to a canal bridge and steps. This adds another 750 metres or so to the walk.]

Cross the next field parallel to the canal and aiming to pass through the small gate on the left of a large metal gate to the right of the farm buildings ahead. Go directly ahead to cross a stile and then follow the left-hand hedge along to reach a further stile in the far left-hand corner. A short enclosed path leads to the last stile by the former Greenhalgh Castle Farm (500m).

The farm is a seventeenth-century building with stone mullion windows. The stone was 'quarried' from the castle that was built to guard the ford over the Wyre in 1490 by the first earl of Derby. This was one of the last strongholds in Lancashire to hold out against Parliament in the Civil War but access to the site is now restricted.

Go left along the farm access road to reach the road bridge over the Wyre. Turn right along the road and then, after some 100 metres and just after the bus shelter, turn right to follow the riverside path back to the start of the walk (1km).

Calder Vale

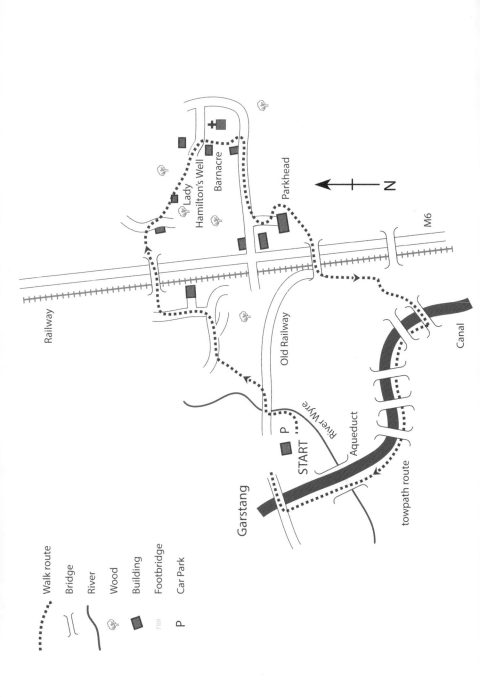

Legend

- Walk route
- Bridge
- River
- Wood
- Building
- Footbridge
- P Car Park

Railway

Lady
Hamilton's Well

Barnacre

Parkhead

M6

N

Garstang

START

P

River Wyre

Old Railway

Aqueduct

Canal

towpath route

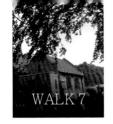

Exploring Barnacre

GARSTANG–BARNACRE–LADY HAMILTON'S WELL–GARSTANG

DISTANCE: 7.6 Kilometres (4.6 miles)

START: Garstang High Street car park (GR 493454)

BUS: Garstang lies on the main Preston to Lancaster route (services 40, 41) and Lancaster to Blackpool Route (services 42 and X42)

PARKING: Pay parking Garstang High Street car park (GR SD493454, PR3 1FA)

MAP: O.S. Explorer OL41 *The Forest of Bowland & Ribblesdale*

TIP: This walk can be done in winter in reasonably dry conditions as well as spring or summer when more wildlife can be seen. Some stiles are challenging for people with limited joint movement. Not all footpaths are signposted off roads or at footpath junctions

A walk along largely dry field paths, quiet lanes and a return along the canal with two heritage features. The walk has elevated viewpoints, especially so when the leaves are off the trees, worthy of the minor efforts of the walk.

From the riverside edge of the car park follow the path along the sports field-edge and riverbank towards the bridge, and climb the steps up the near side of the bridge abutment (400 metres).

The bridge crosses the extraction point from the Lune–Wyre Conjunctive Use Scheme; from here water supplies are piped to

Heron fishing

the Franklaw Treatment Works at Catterall before joining the
North West supply grid. The upstream barriers are to prevent
flood-waters from inundating villages down stream.

Go over the bridge and just after the embankment track has
joined from the left go half-left down steps, pass through the
kissing gate and then across the field to a further kissing gate. In
the next field continue in the same direction to cross a further
kissing gate near the right-hand field corner. Go across the next
field to meet the left-hand boundary, which is followed to a
kissing gate, by a gate, and access to Lingart Lane (500 metres).

Go right along the lane, fork left at the junction, and continue
up to meet the metalled road on a bend and where you turn left.
Follow the road, pass the farm track on your right and, some
50 metres on, at the end of the next field on your right go over
the stiled-footbridge to enter the field. Follow the left-hand
hedge along and then cross the stiled railway footbridge and the
following bridge over the motorway. Continue directly up the
field, go past two lone oak trees, to cross two consecutive stiles
by gates in the top left-hand field corner (1.6km).

On the road go right, pass Crosby Cottage and continue past the
farm buildings until you are nearly opposite the brick built Slack
Farm. Turn left, through a gate, to go down a short enclosed
track to where it crosses a small stream. Cross the stile on the
right and go half-left up this damp field aiming above the trees
to your right to meet a fence. Follow this to your right to cross

a further stile, by the facing wood, into the corner of the field above the fence (500 metres).

In the clump of trees below an alder lies the scant and hidden remains of Lady Hamilton's Well. Hewitson describes this as 'The Spa Well' where the Hamilton family used to bathe when they stayed at Woodacre Hall (no longer standing). Lady Hamilton moved into the area after the death of her husband and perhaps it was her use of this spring-fed well, with its alleged medicinal properties, that has led to its current name. Lady Hamilton was a courtesy title after her love affair with Lord Nelson. In later life she suffered a number of ailments and would certainly have tried spa water treatments.

Climb the steep bank with the wood on your right. Continue directly ahead aiming to the right of the stone house with balcony, pass the well vegetated depression of Delph Quarry down on your right, and go to cross a stile, in the fence, which is a continuation of a stone wall seen to your left. Cross the stile (by a broken small gate) in the lower corner of the field, and continue by the right-hand woodland until you reach a footbridge that enables you to cross the stream and climb the steps to the road outside Barnacre Church (300 metres).

Barnacre Church has interesting stained-glass windows of saints and, if open, is worth looking at inside. Along with Scorton Church it is built to the design of Paley and Austin. The design is austere and appears over solid for a church structure. This is the highest point of the walk and the churchyard seats prove most tempting.

Stained-glass window at
Barnacre Church

From the road outside the lower church gate go up a few stone steps to follow the enclosed path, initially between the

churchyard and house. After two stiles walk ahead for 10 metres
and cross the stile by the second of two consecutive left-hand
gates. When over this, turn right to pass through a small gate
and follow the left-hand fence and enclosed path along to
the end where you leave by a stile to gain a metalled road
(300 metres).

Go right down the metalled Parkhead Lane, immediately passing
Clarkson's farm and when the road divides into three tracks,
take the one to the left. Follow this track along for a short
distance but, before the gateway, turn left and then turn right
to go along the enclosed track. In the field follow the right-hand
boundary down to cross the motorway and subsequent railway
bridge with stiles and gates to pass through. A second, stone
arched former railway bridge over the disused Pilling Pig line is
then crossed (800 metres).

Over this second bridge enter the field (currently through an
open gap) and immediately turn left. In the field gradually bear
away from the left-hand railway-side fence to cross the field,
aiming for the middle of the hedge across your way. In the
next field turn right to follow the right-hand hedge to cross a
largely hidden stile in the far right-hand field corner just beyond
a hedgerow gap. Continue by the right-hand hedge, under the
overhead power lines to a further stile in the right-hand field
corner. Continue ahead to cross the gate in the next right-hand

Wyre aqueduct

field corner then go ahead along the gated track to the bridge over the canal (1.0km).

Go over the bridge and then down the steps on the right and descend to the canal towpath. With the canal to your right-hand go along the towpath to Garstang. The road bridge (number 62) after the aqueduct is where you leave and cross the canal and go through the town centre back to your starting point (2.2km). Perhaps enjoying a cup of tea or ice-cream on your way!

The canal near Garstang

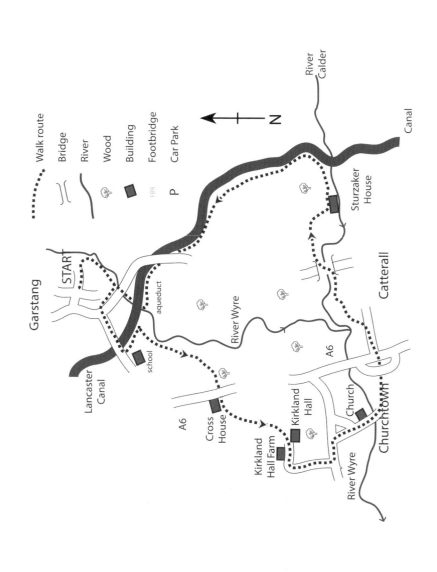

Garstang

START

Lancaster Canal

school

aqueduct

River Wyre

A6

Cross House

Kirkland Hall Farm

Kirkland Hall

Church

River Wyre

Churchtown

A6

Catterall

Sturzaker House

Canal

River Calder

N

Walk route

Bridge

River

Wood

Building

FBR   Footbridge

P   Car Park

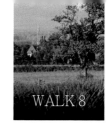

The Wyre's middle reaches: Garstang and Churchtown

GARSTANG–CHURCHTOWN–CATTERALL–GARSTANG

DISTANCE: 9.4 kilometres (5.7 miles)

START: Garstang High Street car park (GR SD 493454)

BUS: Service 42 Blackpool – Garstang links to Churchtown

PARKING: In Garstang High Street car park. (GR SD493454, PR3 1FA)

MAP: *O.S. Explorer OL41 The Forest of Bowland & Ribblesdale*

ROUTE: Garstang to Churchtown section of the Wyre Way is covered (4 km), and is largely well signed

TIP: Lunch can be found in Churchtown (Horns Inn, Punchbowl and Church Rooms, but check opening before starting out!). Good children's playground en route at Catterall

This walk follows the Wyre Way downstream from Garstang to Churchtown and offers excellent views back to the fells of the Forest of Bowland and visits the interesting village of Churchtown.

Go down the side of the Garstang High Street car park to reach the riverbank. Turn right and follow the River Wyre downstream

on a tarmac path that eventually leads out on to the High Street. Turn left and cross the bridge over the river but immediately cross the road and go down the short access to the Cornmill Nursing Home (600 metres).

The blue plaque on the bridge outlines its history.

Pass under the archway of the building and go along the track that once followed the mill-race and go to pass under the aqueduct by the riverbank. Climb the steps on the far side and reach the canal towpath. Cross over the aqueduct, the canal to your right, and walk along for some 80 metres until you find a gated stone gap stile in the left-hand boundary. Here you are almost level with the Tithe Barn canal basin. Leave the towpath through the small gate and cross the school field by the right-hand fence to pass through a kissing gate (400 metres).

The path onwards is called Many Pads and was the main route to St Helen's Church in Churchtown as it was originally the Parish Church for Garstang.

Cross the next field to pass through the next kissing gate and then cross the field to find a stiled footbridge just up from the riverbank. The riverbank is now close to your left and, with houses on your right, a distinct track leads you to a double stile as you aim towards some farm buildings. Climb the steep bank to reach the busy A6 road by a small gate (500 metres).

Go left on the A6 verge but soon carefully cross the road to arrive by the far end of the farm complex. Go through the concrete, gated farm track by the last house and continue along the track to follow alongside a wood until it meets two adjacent

VISITOR CENTRES. If you wish to acquire more information about the landscapes and wildlife you might see on the walks on this book, Wyre Borough Council operates two centres. These are the Discovery Centre, High Street Garstang (01995 602125) and the Wyreside Ecology Centre at Stanah on the Wyre Estuary (01253 857890).

gates. Go left through the left-hand gate and follow the track along the left-hand field boundary until it bends left at the end of the field. Go through the gate facing you and then cross the next field half-right to a gate and stile in the far field corner near the rear of Kirkland Hall. Beyond this is a track which you follow to pass the rear of the Hall, Keepers Cottage and Kirkland Hall Farm and then continue along the farm access road as it bends left to reach the main road just outside Churchtown (1.8 km).

Churchtown

Kirkland Hall has a seven-bay, two and a half storey brick façade built in 1760, but the rear wings contain some seventeenth-century brickwork and date-stones from 1668 and 1695. The Butlers, whose home this once was, were adherents to the House of Stuart and when the King's forces captured Kirkland Hall they took Alexander Butler and his servant as prisoners, on horseback, to Preston. On the journey the servant slipped from his horse and unseated his master into a ditch. The troopers found him more dead than alive and left him to his fate. However he recovered, remounted and returned home.

Cross the A586 to the left and then go down Ainspool Lane, through the middle of the village, passing the market cross and

the Punchbowl Inn to reach St Helen's Church. Continue
through the car park and graveyard extension to reach a small
gate (500 metres).

*St Helen's claims the title of the 'Cathedral of the Fylde' and this
large church is full of interest.
Some of the stonework is
twelfth century and the circular
nature of the original churchyard
suggests it was an earlier,
pagan site. The interior has an
elaborate carved pulpit of 1646,
oak beams donated by Henry
IV from his nearby Myerscough
hunting chase, and rudely carved
miserichords from Cockersand
Abbey (see walk 14 to confirm!).
The church tower is fifteenth
century and the yard has some
plague gravestones and two,
with carvings showing people in
prayer, are referred to as Adam
and Eve. The river once lapped by the church and it has been
suggested that the church owes its origin to Celtic missionaries
who came up the river by coracle.*

St Helen's Church, Churchtown

Through the gate follow the distinct path towards the
footbridge (built in 1985 to replace the suspension bridge
washed away in 1980) and Catterall Hall, one of the oldest
Wyreside houses, on the far bank. Cross the bridge and go
directly ahead to a stile, over which go along a short section of
access track to a cattle grid and various stiles. Over these turn
left and go through the right-hand of two gates (300 metres).

In the field go along the left-hand boundary through two fields
to arrive at a gate and a double stile. Cross the stile, which is
near the meander of the River Wyre, and then go straight ahead

Garstang

to pick up a hard-surfaced track which leads past a house and eventually to a road by a cattle-grid and stile. The houses are on the old A6 (1 km). Along this path look ahead to the fells of Parlick and Fairsnape in the Forest of Bowland area.

Turn right along the road but, on the far side of house number 33, turn left down an enclosed pathway. A former thatched cottage is on your right. This leads to the A6 which you can cross at the island crossing. Go straight down Tan Yard Road with Collinsons industrial complex to your left. Continue on this road

but just before it narrows go left on a surfaced path between some concrete bollards. This

Bridges near Garstang

Near Garstang

path leads you to the River Wyre just short of its confluence with the River Calder. At the end of the building the path turns right and is followed along until the fence on your left bends to the left. Go left here to the bank of the River Calder and this is followed upstream to the road just beyond Catterall play fields and playground (1 km).

Cross the road, turn left over the bridge and them immediately descend to a pair of stiles which admit you into fields. Follow the left-hand boundary along through three fields interconnected by gates and stone gap stiles to reach the next section of road. Turn right along the road which shortly bends left by Sturzacker House Farm, towards the canal bridge. Join the canal bank on the near, right-hand side of the bridge (800 metres).

In summer the towpath is a delight of wildflowers (including flowering rush and bur-reeds), butterflies and a good place to see damsel and dragon flies.

Turn left on the towpath, go under bridge 53, and follow it along back to Garstang. If you leave the canal just after the aqueduct, at bridge 62 the road to the right leads you back into Garstang centre and your starting place (3.3 km).

Female banded demoiselle

Brown hawker dragonfly

Flowering rush

LONGER TRAILS: THE ENGLAND COAST PATH AND THE WYRE WAY. The Wyre Way is the creation of Wyre Borough Council Countryside Service. They have leaflets available on the full route which, they suggest, is a 66 km (41 miles) walking route. The envisaged stages are a Fleetwood and Wyre estuary circular (26 km, 16 miles); Shard Bridge to Garstang (16 km, 10 miles) and Garstang to Tarnbrook/Marshaw (24km, 15 miles). The routes in this book cover most, but not whole of the route, from the source down to the sea.

The Way has much to commend it with the river passing through differing stages with varied, interesting landscapes and with a variety of wildlife, especially birds, to see. Copies of the leaflet can be obtained from local tourist information centres and also as a download from wyre.gov.uk.

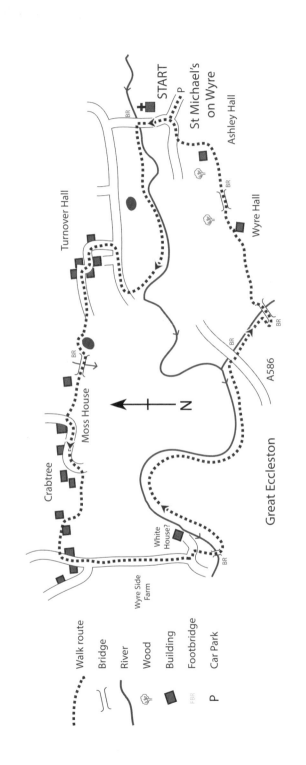

START

St Michael's
on Wyre

P

Ashley Hall

Wyre Hall

BR

Turnover Hall

BR

A586

N

Moss House

Crabtree

BR

White
House?

Wyre Side
Farm

BR

Great Eccleston

Walk route

Bridge

River

Wood

Building

Footbridge

P   Car Park

FBR

The Wyre's middle reaches: St Michael's and Great Eccleston

ST MICHAEL'S ON WYRE–OUT RAWCLIFFE–GREAT ECCLESTON–
ST MICHAEL'S

DISTANCE: 7.8 kilometres (5 miles)

START: St Michael's on Wyre Parish Church (GR 462409)

BUS: Lancaster, Garstang to Poulton and Blackpool 42 service

PARKING: There is a car park just around from the church in Hall Lane (SD462409, PR3 0TQ)

MAP: O.S. Explorer 296 Lancaster, Morecambe and Fleetwood

ROUTE: 4 km of the Wyre Way

TIP: Try this walk out of the summer season

This walk uses a number of less-frequented footpaths in the Fylde and a number of bird species can often be seen. Choose a quiet, sunny winter day with cumulus clouds adding a skyscape to the open views and the fine landscape towards the Forest of Bowland. In early summer watch along the Wyre for the colourful banded demoiselle damselfly. The area gives you the impression of being wooded but the few small woods and the hedgerow trees are actually very thin on the ground.

This section of the Wyre Way rarely sees the river, however more of the river just above its upper tidal limits can be appreciated on our return route. St Michael's Church was said to have been founded between 627 and 640. It was mentioned in the Domesday Survey of 1086. It was rebuilt in 1525 and the church is possibly a mixture of thirteenth-, fifteenth- and sixteenth-century construction.

From St Michael's Church cross the River Wyre by the footbridge and, on the far bank, turn immediately left, cross the road with care, and enter the riverside field by a kissing gate. Follow the river along the embankment top, over a stile, pass the fishing ponds, across another stile and, after some distance, a final stile gives access to Rawcliffe Road. Turn right along the road and turn into the second driveway on the left to Turnover Hall Farm and caravan site (1.5km).

Go down the farm access road which bends left at the bungalow and passes the caravan site reception buildings. Go straight ahead into the farmyard (can be messy when wet and gated) until a range of outbuildings blocks your way and with the house down to the left. Turn right here, go through the gate and then

St Michael's Church

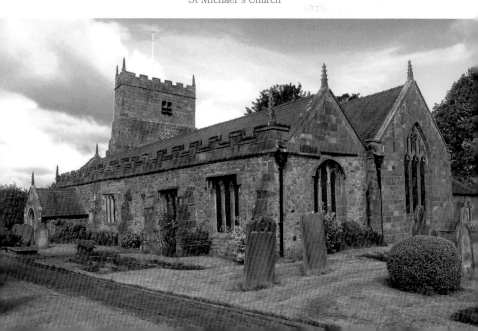

turn immediately left to pass the last buildings through a barrier-type gate and continue directly ahead to leave the yard on a track. Ignore the track off to the right as you continue along a straight track that eventually leads into the right-hand of two adjacent field openings (650 metres).

Go along the field by the track along the left-hand boundary, pass the pond on your left, and continue in the same direction in the next field until, by the left-hand fence, you come to the field corner. Turn left keeping along the fence (the path has boundaries on both sides now) and, shortly, you will find a stile hidden in the right-hand hedge. Over the stile enter the field, go left and continue with the hedge on your left until, along this left-hand boundary, you come to cross a stile by a gate. Turn right in the next field, to continue towards the tower silo of Wild Boar Farm, go over a stile by a gate and then, in the next field, aim for the left-hand of two gates in line with the building to the immediate right of the tower-silo. Wild Boar Farm lies to your right. Cross the stile by this gate, go diagonally left across the farm access track and then enter the field by a stile and gate with the silo on your immediate right (650 metres).

Go directly ahead in the field and leave by a stile and gate in the right-hand field corner by the side of the storage tank. In the next field cross directly towards the building to the right of the bungalow and cross two stiles in short succession to gain access to a farm road. The stiles are some 20 metres to the right of the bungalow. Bear left and then follow the straight track, pass Fir Tree house and go to the track T-junction near the yard of Crabtree Farm. Cross the track junction diagonally left to cross an obvious stile by a gate to re-enter a field (700 metres).

Follow the right-hand field boundary, pass the house, and then leave the field by crossing the stile facing you in the far right-hand field corner. Continue by the right-hand boundary in the next field and leave it by a further stile by a gate in the boundary facing you by the field corner. Here you leave the Wyre Way.

Turn left down the track, pass by the farm buildings and go to meet the metalled road by Wyre Side Farm. Turn left on the road and, after 200 metres, go right to cross the footbridge beyond the aqueduct bridge (900 m).

Here the River Wyre has almost thrown off the faint whiff of sea salt as you now follow the upper tidal reaches of the river.

Over the river turn left on the riverside embankment and, after five stiles by gates and a final stile, you emerge on the side of the A586 Road (2 km).

This section of the walk has great views towards the Bowland Fells, Beacon Fell and Longridge Fell. The village of Great Eccleston could be reached by any of the paths leading right from the embankment.

Cross the road with care and then the facing stile. Go along the drain-side embankment (although stiles are provided at the base of the embankment) through two fields until the dyke is bridged. Cross the gated bridge and then walk diagonally left to cross a stile where the left-hand hedge kinks. In the next field follow the right-hand boundary and, after a stile by a gateway with stone gate posts, continue directly ahead by the right-hand

River Wyre by Great Eccleston

Tansy growing by the River Wyre at Great Eccleston

boundary to cross the stile by a gate immediately facing you in front of the houses (800 metres).

Go diagonally left to cross the access track to enter a field by the obvious stile, which faces the front of the white-painted Wyre Hall house. Walk by the right-hand boundary, cross the stile by the water trough and then go along the right-hand boundary and pass through the gate facing you in the corner of this small field. In the next, larger field go parallel to the left-hand wood to reach and cross the footbridge in the boundary facing you. Cross the next field, in the same direction to a stile, over which go left. Go down this track for some 20–30 metres to meet a gate. [An alternate route back would be to continue on this track to the main road, turn right and follow the pavement back to your starting point. Turn right in front of the gate, pass by the small, unfenced copse and then follow the left-hand ditch and hedge along the left-hand edge of the field. Cross the stile in the far left-hand field corner and continue along the left-hand boundary to cross a further stile by the gate facing you. At the entrance gates to Ashley Hall turn left down the lane to reach the main road and your starting point is to the right (1.4km).

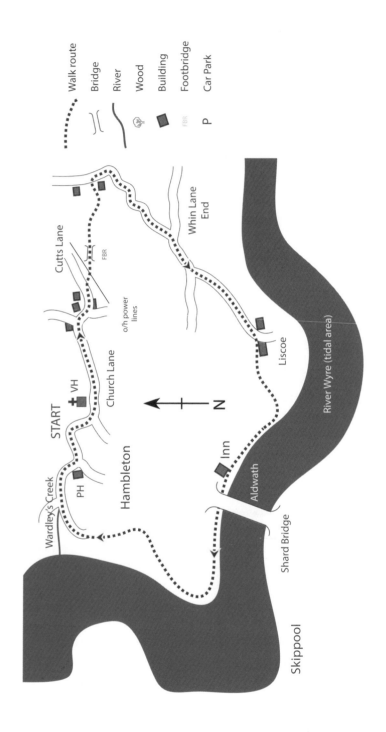

Walk route

Bridge

River

Wood

Building

Footbridge

P   Car Park

FBR

START

Wardley's Creek

PH

Hambleton

VH

Church Lane

Cutts Lane

FBR

o/h power lines

Whin Lane End

N

Liscoe

Inn

Aldwath

Shard Bridge

River Wyre (tidal area)

Skippool

Down to the Saltings

HAMBLETON–OUT RAWCLIFFE–ALDWATH–HAMBLETON

DISTANCE: 7 kilometres (4.5 miles)

START: Centre of Hambleton village by The Shovels public house (GR 371424)

BUS: 89 Lancaster to Poulton services to Hambleton – alight at The Shovels. 2C Blackpool to Knott End service also goes through Hambleton

PARKING: Polite street parking in Hambleton (FY6 9BX)

MAP: O.S. Explorer 296 *Lancaster, Morecambe and Fleetwood*

ROUTE: Some 3.8 km of rough walking along the Wyre Way is included in this route

TIP: This walk is occasionally wet and is well vegetated but it does cover a floristically rich section of saltmarsh, which is the route of the Wyre Way. Late June to early August show the rich flowers and butterflies but, given the nature of the vegetation growth in some fields and on the saltmarsh it may be more easily undertaken as a winter, early spring walk. In any case do not attempt the saltmarsh footpaths when there are high tides of 9 metres as some parts of this walk may be underwater. Bird life on the estuary can also be rewarding viewing. There are a few sections of quiet country roads to walk

From Hambleton's The Shovels public house go along the main road (Broadpool Lane) in the direction of Pilling, cross the zebra crossing towards the small terrace of shops and then turn right,

Common emerald

in front of Ryecroft Hall into Carr Lane, and its continuation, Sandy Lane. Walk the length of this road and turn left into Church Lane. Follow this past the Bob Williamson playing fields on your right and then school and church on your left until it meets Ghants Lane at a T-junction. Turn right, and then almost immediately left into Cutts Lane (1.3km).

Go along Cutts Lane, pass Moss Side Farm on your left and, when under the overhead power lines, cross the stile by the first gate on your right to enter a field and to face a cluster of high voltage transmission towers. Go left in the field, pass diagonally under the high voltage overhead wires and then walk parallel to the right-hand boundary to go to cross a stiled footbridge in the boundary facing you. Go up the next long field to cross a stile in the top right-hand field corner. Cross the next stile shortly ahead from where an enclosed path leads to a further stile and the road (900 metres).

Turn right down the road, and eventually right again (into Whin Lane) at the T-junction. When this road bends go left down a cul-de-sac road. At the entrance to Rawcliffe Hall the metalled road becomes a rougher track which leads you to the house and yard of Liscoe Farm (1.3 km).

Where the rougher track starts you have joined the Wyre Way. The core of the farmhouse is probably of seventeenth-century construction.

Just beyond the farmhouse the track bends left into the farmyard. However, continue directly ahead, along a gated track whilst keeping all the farm buildings to your left and then enter the field by the double gate ahead. Follow the left-hand boundary down the long field, at one stage passing a pond on your right, to reach and pass through the kissing gate by the gate in the facing boundary near the bottom corner of the field. In the next field continue directly ahead by the relic hedge but, just before you reach the end of the field with its embankment, go right to aim for the field corner where you climb the embankment and go through a gate (600 metres).

Sea lavender

Go along the embankment and continue until the way is blocked by a hawthorn shrub and there is a stile on your right. Do not cross this stile but drop down left to the saltings, then turn right to follow the path in tall, rough vegetation along to pass the Shard Bridge Hotel and arrive under the right-hand arch of the new Shard Bridge (900 metres).

On your way you have passed the site of the old Shard Bridge which itself occupied the location of an ancient river crossing Aldwath (the old ford), known from at least 1330. The replacement toll-free bridge opened in 1993. Some of the local boulder clay deposits, besides the river, show rocks that came from the Lake District via glaciers.

Continue from under the bridge along the edge of the saltings to follow the River Wyre. The huge sweep of Skippool is best seen when the tide levels permit sailing to take place. After the prominent right-hand gate of Bank Farm go up and along the embankment top towards the houses at Hambleton. At the far end of a block of flats the main route continues on the saltmarsh edge until you can climb and follow the surfaced track that leads you to a road by Wardleys Creek (1.7 km).

Looking over the River Wyre to Hambledon

The former Shard toll bridge

This is where a ferry once crossed the Wyre to Cockle Hall and is the site of an historic harbourage. (Just on the far side of these flats a further path turns right and is enclosed between fences. This leads quickly back to the road near The Shovels.)

On reaching the road on the near side of Wardley's Creek go to the right on the road (Kiln Lane) as it bends right and brings us back to the start at The Shovels (300 metres).

Wardleys Creek, now popular with small boat enthusiasts, was an early harbourage and shipbuilding site. In the early nineteenth century several emigrant ships left here for the Americas.

The name of the river, the Wyre, is taken by the local district council. It is possibly a Celtic derivative of the Welsh 'Gwyar' meaning blood water, a possible description of the reddish-brown peat load carried by the river in spate. The river rises in the Bowland fells above Abbeystead before flowing to the sea in Morecambe Bay between Fleetwood and Knott End.

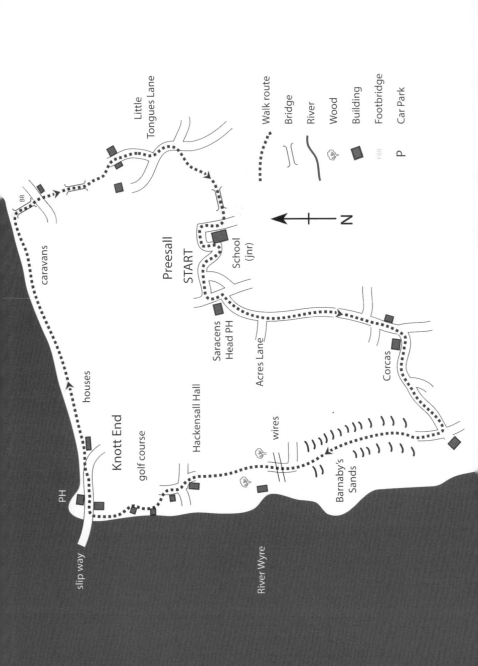

Little
Tongues Lane

Walk route

Bridge

River

Wood

Building

Footbridge

FBR

P   Car Park

N

BR

caravans

Preesall

START

School
(jnr)

Saracens
Head PH

Acres Lane

Corcas

Knott End

golf course

Hackensall Hall

wires

houses

PH

slip way

Barnaby's
Sands

River Wyre

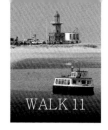

Amongst the salt mines

KNOTT END–PREESALL–WYRE ESTUARY–KNOTT END

DISTANCE: 10.5 km (6 miles)

START: Knott End by ferry slipway (GR 346485). The walk could also be started in Preesall

BUS: Services 89 Lancaster to Knott End or 2C Blackpool to Knott End

FERRY: Service from Fleetwood to Knott End

PARKING: Car Park by Knott End Golf Club (SD 346485, FY6 0AA)

MAP: *O.S. Explorer 296: Lancaster, Morecambe and Fleetwood*

ROUTE: 3.5 km of the Wyre Way along the Wyre estuary to Knott End; 2km of the England Coast Path to the east of Knott End

TIP: A good walk in summer when the sea lavender is in flower

This walk explores the Wyre Estuary and the southern fringe of Morecambe Bay. The route goes through the former brine fields and alongside a nature reserve on the Wyre estuary. The last stage of the Wyre Way and a small part of the England Coast Path are described. It is a good walk to see wading and other birds and some interesting wild flowers. At the start is a fitting sculpture to

Knott End Lowry

*L. S. Lowry and suggests where the artist painted the Wyre Ferry.
The name Knott End is curious and it may have been the last site
of a series of river marker posts (knots or cairns) set by the Norse
settlers. The offshore large sandbank was named after St Bernard.*

Walk along the road (Bourne May Road) away from the slipway
and just after the Bourne Arms follow the promenade path
along the shore of Morecambe Bay. Continue to the seaward
side of the houses as the path then follows the sea defence wall.
After the last houses the path passes Brookfield House caravan
site and, almost immediately the next, Sandy Bay, caravan site (2
km).

Leave the sea wall by the right-hand steps immediately after
the second of these caravan sites, descend to a path which
is followed, with the caravans on your right, to reach a road.
Cross the road diagonally left to a track with a stile, alongside
a gate adjacent to the house, that leads to Huckleberry's Pre-
School. When the track bends left go along the short enclosed
footpath directly ahead. Follow this path to a stile to enter a
field. Continue, with two further stiles, through the next fields

keeping by the right-hand dyke (Wheal Foot Watercourse). Continue ahead when a footbridge crosses the dyke to the bungalows on your right and cross the next footbridge directly ahead. Continue by the right-hand dyke, with three further stiles by gates, to emerge onto a track. Bear left on the track and then right as this becomes Little Tongue's Lane to reach a main road by Preesall Garage (1.6 km).

Turn left along the road, cross when safe and continue to a bus stop sign on a lamp-post just after the white bungalow, Pennine View. Leave the road here to follow the enclosed path to cross a stile then go immediately left to cross the next, obvious, stile in the fenced field corner. Then bear right to go to cross the footbridge. Climb the steep slope ahead and go through the small gate at the rear of the school grounds. Looking back, the vista of the Bowland hills and the Fylde plain is worth a rest. Follow to the right the meandering enclosed path, around the school grounds, and from the school entrance go right down School Lane to reach the main road just up from the Black Bull pub (800 metres).

A pile of horse shoes near Preesall

Go left from the Black Bull along the main road but soon turn right down Back Lane. Continue to pass Acres Lane on the right and then, after some distance, Cemetery Lane on the left. Continue along Back Lane to pass semi-detached cottages, go over a bridged dyke and, shortly after, Corcas Farm marks where you turn right and go down an enclosed track (marked private road and bridle path). Follow this past the farm and all the way until it meets the metalled road end by the collection of bungalows at The Heads (2.6km).

At The Heads the Wyre Way comes along the road from the left. On your way the lane has interesting hedgerows, provides views of the stump of Preesall's windmill and, on more open parts as it meanders amongst the drumlins, views east to the Forest of Bowland where lie the headwaters of the Wyre.

Turn right here, by the Wyre Way signpost and go along the short track to climb the stile by the gate and then walk the length of the embankment beyond until it ends by a track (1.5km).

The land to the left is Barnaby's Sands, a Site of Special Scientific Interest (SSSI). This SSSI is an ungrazed saltmarsh, which along with nearby Burrow's Marsh, forms a unique wildlife resource in the county. Although the nitrate- and phosphate-rich waters of the estuary have encouraged the invasion of cord grass (Spartina)

A pair of Shelduck

Wardleys Creek over the River Wyre to Hambleton

since the 1940s the zonation of vegetation and the occurrence
of some flowers such as the unique rock sea lavender make this
a fascinating comparison with grazed saltmarshes. Sea beet,
glasswort, sea lavender, sea aster and sea radish can be seen,
along with birds such as oystercatcher, curlew, shelduck and
lapwing at various times of the year. These marshes provide wader
and wildfowl roosts and therefore walkers need to minimise any
disturbance by keeping to the path.

The area to the right of the embankment is the Preesall saltfield
that was re-discovered in 1872 during prospecting for iron ore.
The remains of the old salt-mining industry are notable through
ponds occupying collapsed mines. This former inland sea from
some 210 million years ago evaporated leaving salt which was
mined by pumping in water, the brine being used across the
river at a soda works. When rock salt was mined as a solid it
was known for its quality. The rock salt occurs in 120 metre thick
beds and is exceptionally hard – originally it was mined with the

help of blasting. The first sample of salt was produced after the prospectors returned to their lodgings and their landlady dissolved, filtered and evaporated the water to produce the mineral.

A mine was opened and salt was taken by a small railway along the track you have now reached, to the estuary side where it was shipped out to Australia, South America, the Baltic countries, Canada, India, Burma and Iceland. The few well-head markers show where water was used to dissolve the salt and the brine produced pumped out. This left salt pillars between the wells and avoided ground collapse that was once a major problem but created the interesting ponds in the area.

Salt was known in the area earlier as some of the local names reflect and there are records from the fifteenth to the eighteenth centuries of the evaporation of sea water in the locality.

From the end of the embankment go directly ahead on the track, continue past some small, windswept woods, over the lower reaches of the golf course and arrive at the track junction by the side of Hackensall Hall (1km).

The name of the hall is derived from the Viking personal name Haakon who probably settled in the area in the ninth or early tenth century. The hall was built by Richard and Anne Fleetwood of Rossall in 1656 as their original house site was vulnerable to flooding. There may have been an earlier moated house on the site. During a nineteenth-century renovation it is rumoured that two concealed skeletons were found in walls. There are stories of the house being haunted by a horse. A hoard of around 500 Roman Coins was found nearby in 1926.

Go left at the track junction, bending to keep all the buildings to your left, and re-enter the golf course immediately after some of their ground-maintenance buildings. Follow the path directly across the narrow part of the golf course to head for the prominent green shed. With the estuary and Fleetwood now below you to the left go along the edge of the course and

bear left immediately after the cottage (Sea Dyke) to reach the riverside embankment. Go along the embankment to the ferry slipway and the cafés and toilets of Knott End (1km).

One story says that the Norse people marked the navigable channel of the river by cairns or knotts, with the final one being Knott End. The terminal station for the railway, which arrived in Knott End in 1908, was situated where the café (near the golf clubhouse) now stands.

THE ENGLAND COAST PATH From 2021 most of the English coast will have a continuous coastal footpath with additional coastal access called spreading room. This book is published before the final route through the area has been determined, but three walks (11, 12 & 13) do include sections of this route.

Wyre ferry at Knott End

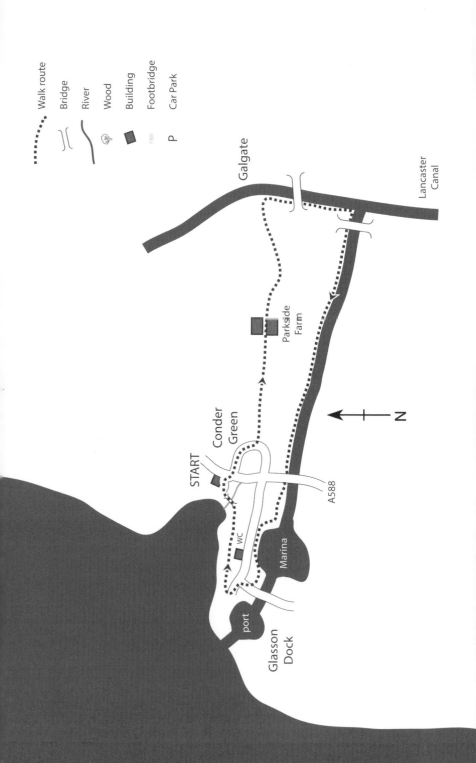

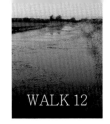
When canals and railways held sway

CONDER GREEN–THE GLASSON CANAL BRANCH–GLASSON DOCK

DISTANCE: 9.2 kilometres (5.5 miles) – with two extensions suggested at the end of the described route

START: Conder Green Picnic Site (GR SD456561). Alternately starts could be made from Glasson Dock (GR 445562) or Galgate (GR SD483550)

BUS: 89 Lancaster to Knott End also stops by Conder Green Stork Inn

PARKING: This is inexpensive and readily available at Conder Green (SD456561, LA2 0AN) or in Glasson Dock

MAP: O.S. Explorer 296: Lancaster, Morecambe and Fleetwood

TIP: A good walk in summer when there is more activity and wildlife to be seen along the canal. See also walk 14

This walk gently explores part of a series of drumlins that stretch from Kendal to Preston, down towards Garstang by quiet field paths, before using the canal to reach Glasson Dock. The old railway track returns us to Conder Green. The walk therefore features transport through the ages and there is often much wildlife to see, especially along the canal and by the Lune estuary. There are refreshments available at Conder Green, Galgate and Glasson Dock.

Glasson Dock

From Conder Green car park go down the access road from the Café d'Lune and join the main A588 at the Stork Hotel. Turn right and carefully go along the main road until the first turning on the left can be seen. Go down this side road and when it forms a T-junction by the buildings enter the field by the stepped stile found on the right of the electricity substation (750 metres).

Follow the right-hand boundary up the first field and then through the gate directly head. Continue along the right-hand hedge and go down to cross a stile in the bottom right-hand corner of the field and adjacent to Crow Wood. Immediately cross a small footbridge and then turn left to go through a gated stile. Follow the left-hand hedge up the next two fields, connected by a stile and gate, and emerge through the stile and gate into the yard of Parkside Farm (1km).

Cross the farm track directly ahead, pass through the farmyard and, by a further gate, enter a field. Go up this field by the right-hand hedge but, before you reach the pylon ahead, go right through the stile by the gate. Turn left in this next field and go down by the left-hand hedge and then up a slight rise to find a kissing gate in the far left-hand corner of the original hedged field (400 metres).

Glasson Branch bridge

Climb this last drumlin directly, gradually moving away from the left-hand hedge. When on the highest point (the last climb of the walk!) descend to pass through a kissing gate to enter the Forerigg Wood. The path descends distinctly through the wood and then a stile takes you into a field. Go right, along the edge of the wood, over a stile by a gate and, and cross this last field before the canal towpath, by aiming for a white building to cross a stile which admits you to the towpath of the Lancaster Canal (400 metres).

The Lancaster Canal ran from Preston to Tewitfield for forty-eight kilometres before the first and only flight of locks on the way to Kendal was reached. The bridges you pass under are fine half-elliptical arches, examples of the work of the canal builder John Rennie. One bridge, number 87, is a small but perfectly formed example of Rennie's architecture and this is where the canal crosses the River Conder by an aqueduct.

Go right along the towpath (bridge 86 admits you to Galgate and possible refreshments) until you come to the junction with the Glasson Branch canal (1.5km).

Thurnham, Glasson Branch

Turn right by the fine arched bridge to follow the Glasson branch all the way down to Glasson Dock (4km).

From Glasson Dock go to the estuary side at the rear of the public toilets near the Victoria Hotel and, with the estuary on your left, walk along the route of the old railway and modern flood defences to reach your start at Conder Green (1.15km).

If you continue through Conder Green car park and picnic site (the route is now labelled The River Lune Millennium Park), as with the suggested longer routes below, you are on the trackbed of the railway line from Lancaster to Glasson Dock which opened in 1890 and carried passenger services until 1930. It closed to freight in 1947 but the tracks were not raised until 1962. The only claim to fame of the line was in 1917 when King George V slept overnight on the royal train at Glasson. Trains to the dock were notorious for shaking a row of cottages near the port.

Tales were told of railway firemen who used to kick out lumps of coal from their cabs when passing a fisherman's hut. Sometimes an exchanged salmon made the return journey. One engine driver was demoted after arriving at Lancaster only to discover that his carriages had been left behind at Glasson Dock station!

There was a station at Conder Green and a private one used by Lord Ashton at Ashton Hall where you can still find the overgrown remains of the timber platform. Birdwatchers will need binoculars along this estuary-side path.

TWO SUGGESTED LONGER ROUTES

1. This extension walk can be started at Lancaster. From Lancaster go to join the canal towpath to the south of the city centre and then continue as in the above walk and return to Lancaster following the railway route from Conder Green along to St George's Quay into Lancaster. This route is 21 kilometres (13 miles).

2. Starting from Conder Green, follow the railway line north to the former railway crossing and road end below Aldcliffe, walk up the road through the settlement, at the top of the village go left at the road junction and follow the road down to meet the canal. The canal is then followed to the right (south) to join the above route. This route is 16 kilometres (10 miles).

Conder Green, Glasson Dock

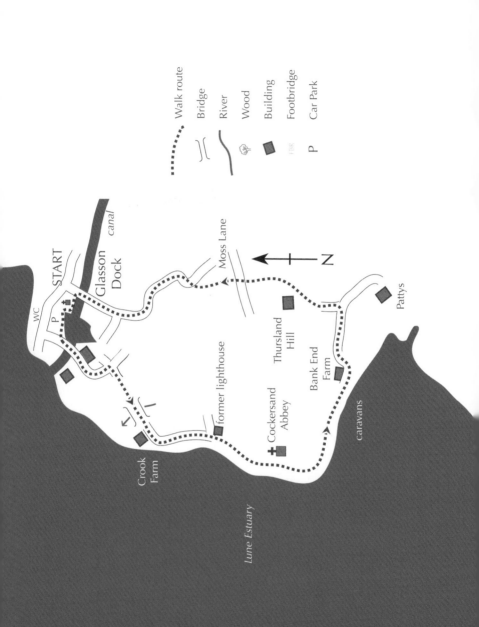

START

Glasson Dock

canal

WC

P

Crook Farm

former lighthouse

Moss Lane

N

Thursland Hill

Bank End Farm

Cockersand Abbey

caravans

Pattys

Lume Estuary

Walk route

Bridge

River

Wood

Building

Footbridge

P   Car Park

Exploring the Lune estuary

GLASSON DOCK–COCKERSAND ABBEY–GLASSON DOCK

DISTANCE: 9.5 kilometres (6 miles)

START: Glasson Dock

BUS: Glasson Dock is served by the 89 Lancaster to Knott End buses.

PARKING: Pay and display in Glasson Dock opposite public toilets (GR SD445561, LA2 0DB)

MAP: *O.S. Explorer 296: Lancaster, Morecambe and Fleetwood*

ROUTE: This route covers some 5.5 km (3.5 miles) of the England Coast Path and, should the Ramblers' suggestions be taken up, the walk may have a more coastal feel between Glasson Dock and Crook Farm from 2021

TIP: Refreshments are available in Glasson Dock as are public toilets. A good walk for wildlife in any season. Some of the field paths may be easier to walk after silage harvesting is finished. Take your binoculars in winter especially when the tides are flowing in

This walk has a variety of interests, especially the most wild section of the Morecambe Bay coast by the Lune estuary. Glasson Dock is largely a product of the canal age and developed when

the increasing size of ships and silting of the Lune prevented ships using St George's Quay in Lancaster. The main dock was constructed by 1791 and was large enough to hold 25 large merchant ships. Some of the trade was with the West Indies. The branch canal was opened to the dock in 1826 and is notable for its wooden lock footbridges and the side weirs at the locks. The railway link with Lancaster took away the canal trade but today the port is still used commercially. The village relies to some degree on tourism – especially at weekends and Bank Holidays.

From the lock swingbridge, by the port, follow the road up Tithebarn Hill to the viewpoint with an indicator and fine views across the estuary to Sunderland. The views are extensive and cover 360 degrees. Turn left on the road at the top and then go right, into Marsh Lane, at the next crossroads near the farm with two prominent silo towers. Go down the enclosed lane and pass through a gate just beyond the caravan site entrance (550 metres).

After passing through a gate follow the path through the field, initially by the remnants of the right-hand hedge line, then bear left to pass over a gated bridge that takes you over a dyke before you continue along the track by a further right-hand hedge to reach, by a gated enclosed track, the rear of Crook Farm. Go through the gate and pass to the left of the farm buildings and then follow the farm access road to the left, along the Lune estuary, to a road junction by Lighthouse Cottage (1.75km).

The area of the Lune and Cocker estuaries is a bird sanctuary and in winter can provide a spectacle of many thousands of waders. The embankment itself is rich in wild flowers – many seaside species which, in turn, offer summer nectar to insects, particularly butterflies. It is a good place to learn to recognise coastal plants. The estuaries of the Lune and Wyre, in Morecambe Bay, are designated Marine Conservation Zones.

From left to right: sea bindweed; sea campion; thrift; sea holly

Continue along the estuary-side track, go through a kissing gate by a gate, along the edge of the sea defence wall and, after a further kissing gate, you are able to reach the ruin of Cockersand Abbey (800 m).

The remains of Cockersand Abbey consist almost entirely of the Chapter House. The site was established by the Premonstratensian Order in 1190, and was previously the abode of hermit Hugh Garth in 1180 – possibly then on an island site – before it became a hospital colony for lepers and the infirm. Dissolution came in 1539 when the house contained 22 priests, five aged and infirm men who were 'kept dayle of charitie', and 57 servants. The Chapter House (c.1230), with its vaulted roof held by clustered columns and leafy capitals, later became a burial vault for the Dalton family of Thurnham Hall. The Daltons were probably responsible for the crenellation.

Cockersand Abbey

Keep by the seaward edge of the field and, just before the wartime look out building, descend by a concrete ramp to a small gate and the road at Bank House. Keep on the edge of the foreshore to the road end at Cockerham Sands caravan park and then continue on the seaward edge, via a small gate to eventually reach a tarred road at Bank End Farm (1.5km).

Go ahead to follow the road beside the embankment (which can also be used) to the road junction (900 m). Here we leave the England Coast Path.

Turn left at the T-junction, by the memorial seat, and as the road is bending right leave by the track in the left-hand corner of the road bend. Follow this rough-surfaced track until a gate crosses your way. Turn right on the nearside of this gate and go through the adjacent gate and go along the enclosed track until you meet a further gate. Through this gate go along the right-hand field boundary until another gate crosses your path. Through the gate cross the middle of the next field heading for the farm complex ahead until, on the far side of the field, you pick up a left-hand boundary which takes you to a further gate which you pass through. Continue along the left-hand hedge and when this turns left follow it to pass through a gate in the field corner (1.2 km).

The farm is called Thursland Hill but locally it is pronounced Thor's land after a putative viking settlement on the higher land which, at the time, may have been a tidal island. Before this the island

Plover Scar lighthouse

Across the Lune to Sunderland Point

feature was probably occupied by Stone Age people as stone axes are reputed to have been found here.

Through this gate go to turn right with a shack, caravan and pond to your left and follow down this enclosed section of path to a double-stiled footbridge in the hedge facing you. Cross this, ignore the next stile to the right, and continue in the field along the right-hand hedge to reach a further footbridge in the far right-hand corner which gives you access to a metalled road (500 m).

Cross the road diagonally right to the second of two almost adjacent gates (the end of the track has a sign with an M) to re-enter a field. Follow the left-hand hedge along this long, narrow field to a gate in the far left-hand corner through which you continue to follow the left-hand hedge in the second field. Just after a stile on your left you come to a gate (it may be easier to use the stile than the gate) which gives access to the next field. Walk across this field, immediately you are parallel to the right-hand boundary but go to find a gate in the far right-hand corner of the field. In this last field turn left to follow the boundary and continue when it bends right where you see the Bowland Fells ahead. This leads to a stile and a metalled road (1.2 km).

Turn left on the road, continue straight ahead at the junction to the canal bridge. Go down from this bridge to the canal towpath and, with the canal on your left, you are soon back at your start in Glasson Dock (1km).

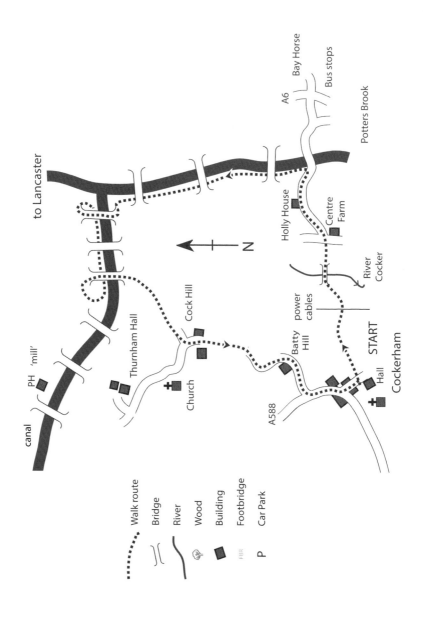

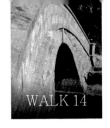

Cockerham and the canal junction

COCKERHAM–GLASSON JUNCTION–COCKERHAM

DISTANCE: 8.3 kilometres (5.2 miles)

START: Cockerham centre (GR 465523). Alternatively bus passengers from Garstang and the south can alight at Bay Horse/Potters Brook but only for the longer route

BUS: Cockerham is served by the 89 Lancaster to Knott End buses. Bay Horse/Potters Brook is on the Lancaster–Garstang–Preston Service 40 & 41 route and the 42 Lancaster to Blackpool via Garstang service

PARKING: In Cockerham near Parish Hall (LA2 0EF)

MAP: *O.S. Explorer 296: Lancaster, Morecambe and Fleetwood*

TIP: This walk has a variety of interests especially the most scenic sections of the Lancaster Canal. There is one stretch, between Cock Hill and Batty Hills farms, which can be wet after heavy rain but nonetheless, it is a walk for all seasons

From Manor Inn in the centre of Cockerham walk south along Main Street and turn left onto the footpath immediately adjacent to house number 27. Go through the short garden, pass the rear of the houses and climb the stile at the top. In the field follow the right-hand hedge up the hillock, a drumlin (200 metres).

From this rise there are extensive views of Wyresdale, Morecambe Bay, the Lakeland Fells and south towards Winter Hill. The hillocks are all drumlins, post glacial deposits, that stretch between Kendal and Preston.

Descend the hillock to cross a stile where the right-hand hedge kinks at the base of the hillock. Now follow the hedge on your left and cross a stile by a gate facing you just right of the field corner. Cross the next field diagonally right to the gate and stiled footbridge in the far right-hand corner, by the corner of a small wood. In the next field follow the left-hand hedge, pass under the overhead power line and cross a footbridge over the River Cocker in the field corner (700 metres).

Small tortoiseshell

Follow up the right-hand edge of the wood, pass through a gateway and go over the stile almost immediately on your right. Go up the next field along the left-hand hedge and through the gate facing you by the top left-hand field corner. Diagonally cross the middle of the next field to pass through a gate at the rear of the outbuildings of Centre Farm (450 metres). Follow the track ahead, with the farm buildings on your right. The enclosed track passes Holly House Farm and then leads down to the canal (1.1km).

Those using the bus along the A6 at Bay Horse/Potters Brook will join and leave the walk here. The bus stop is a short distance over the canal bridge.

Follow the canal northwards, water on your right, until it comes to the high-arched bridge over the Glasson branch (2 km).

The canal stretch has adjacent woods, a rock-cutting through the local sandstone to an attractive canal junction and has boating activity and wildlife along the way. The Lancaster canal runs between the 50 and 100 foot contours and was built following a 1792 Act of Parliament. Its main users were industrial, agricultural and passenger traffic. Boats carried cargoes of coal north from

The canal bridge at Ellel Grange

Wigan and limestone south from Kendal. The bridges are the typical elliptical design of the builder, John Rennie. However, two bridges we pass under are slightly different in design. Bridge 84 (access track to Ellel Grange) was modified by adding balusters to the sides thus forming an ornamental parapet. Bridge 85 is called Double Bridge due to its width. The tracks over, now only a footpath, are kept separate and it was said this was due to the two adjoining landowners not being on the best of terms and refusing to share a single bridge.

At the canal junction cross the bridge and turn down left to follow the Glasson Branch of the canal (see walk 12). At lock three go under the white-railed bridge and then pass through the gap stile by the gate immediately on your right. Use the track beyond to cross bridge 3 (900 m). After the gate and stile on the bridge follow the distinct farm track through the fields, under the overhead power line, through Cock Hall Wood and reach, via several gates, the yard of Cock Hall Farm (900 m).

Pass the farm buildings to your left (a new house is on the right), cross the farm access track and go down to a small gate by the far corner of the barn. Enter the field and go left alongside the farm buildings until you pass under an overhead power lines with a pole-mounted transformer. Turn half-right to go down the field, gradually moving further from the overhead power line, to cross a stiled footbridge in the hedge facing you. In this next field aim to the right of the farm complex ahead and leave the field by a gate in the far right-hand field corner. This gives access to a track (largely enclosed and often very wet) which leads up to Batty Hill Farm. The farm access road then leads down to the main A588 road where, by turning left, you are back at the start of your walk (please take care on the road) (2.1 km).

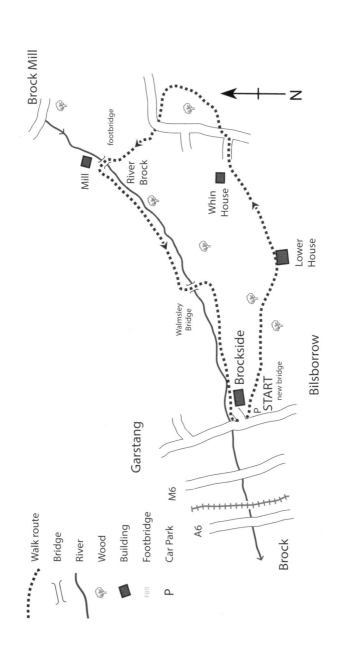

Walk route

Bridge

River

Wood

Building

Footbridge FBR

P Car Park

Brock Mill

footbridge

Mill

River Brock

Whin House

Walmsley Bridge

Lower House

Garstang

Brockside

START

new bridge

Bilsborrow

M6

A6

Brock

N

The secretive River Brock

NEW BRIDGE–BROCK BOTTOMS–NEW BRIDGE

DISTANCE: 7.2 kilometres (4.5 miles) or for bus users an extra 2 km

START: New Bridge, Lydiate Lane (GR 523410). Public transport users can start at Brock (GR 512406)

BUS: Service 40 & 41 Lancaster–Garstang–Preston service to Brock – alight near garage, walk through car showroom car park to bridge over railway. Follow river upstream to New Bridge and return on same route. This adds 2km in total to the walk

PARKING: A few roadside spaces at New Bridge on Lydiate Lane (Bilsborrow parish) (GR SD 523410, PR3 0GL)

MAP: O.S. Explorer OL41 *The Forest of Bowland & Ribblesdale*

TIP: A good walk to do in early spring or when the leaves have turned in autumn as this will give you better views of the river which is secreted behind the riverside trees

The middle and upper reaches of the River Brock are a long-time favourite area for Lancashire ramblers. Much of the river can be followed close to its banks; there is delightful scenery and good opportunities of seeing river birds such as dipper, wagtails or kingfisher but, as its banks are well wooded, the river often has a secretive appearance. Some of the paths can be very muddy, and some of the fields on the return route can be damp. The walk is an excellent stroll along the river, especially in autumn when the

A young wren

riverside woodlands are at their best but the open fields give good prospects of the coast and the fells above Bleasdale.

From New Bridge walk south, passing the entrance to the houses of Badger's Wood, along a short stone wall on your left which ends by a gate. Go through the gate, into this small field, and head half-right to cross a stile in the next hedge. In the next, large field go half-left heading to the right of Beacon Fell. Views of Fairsnape and Bleasdale fells open up on this outward route. The path meets the left-hand hedge at a corner where you cross a stile and follow the right-hand hedge of the next field to reach the first gate on your right. Through this gate turn left and follow the obvious farm track along though several fields and gates until you are almost at Lower House farm (1.5 km). [The actual public right of way cuts half-right after passing through the first, double gates on this track and re-meets the tracks via a stile just short of the farm.]

Before you enter the farm complex go left through a metal gate, turn right in the field to cross a stile behind the farm, go through a small wood and leave by the small gate at the top. Go left along the track but, when it bends sharp left, continue directly ahead through a gate and stile to enter a wood-top track. Follow this track along its full length to cross a stile and emerge by Winn House Farm. Below you, to the right, is a typical Lancashire clough woodland albeit infested with sycamore (900 metres).

Descend right in front of the house to the farm access track which is followed up to the metalled road. Go left on the road but, after around 30 metres, leave it by a double stile on your right. Follow the right-hand hedge up the field but when a relic hedge, the scant remains of a former field boundary, meets from the left turn left just beyond the hedge line and gradually walk away from it and aiming to cross a stile by an obvious gate in the boundary ahead (300 metres).

In the next field aim for the far right-hand corner but, before the corner is reached, go right and cross a stile by a gate. In this next large field cross half-left whilst aiming for the white farm building with Beacon Fell behind it. When you come to a stile in the fence across your way turn left in front the stile and follow along the right-hand boundary to the gate in the field corner. On the nearside of this gate turn left and continue along the right-hand boundary to a further gate and stile. Over this stile follow the track along to the gate and the metalled road (800 metres).

From the slight elevation views to the coast are extensive.

Go right on the road which soon bends to the right. Leave the road on this corner by the footpath on the left. This track goes through a wood, rakes down steeply towards the river, and eventually bears right in a glade and leads to a footbridge over the River Brock (600 metres).

The River Brock

Over the bridge and to the right was the site of Brock Bottoms Mill and hamlet but the foundations are now difficult to see. Your path down to the river was probably an access route to the mill and also probably an old packhorse route. The mill had many reincarnations. It was originally a corn mill or paper mill and, around 1791, became an Arkwright-machinery cotton mill. After a serious fire in 1860 it was rebuilt to make rollers for cotton spinning machines but later in life saw the production of files for metalworkers until it closed in 1936. After this time it served briefly as a café with, on Saturday nights, dancing to the Calder Vale Band.

Over the bridge our way is to the left along an obvious track. When this begins to bend right and climb there is a small and large metal gate in front of you. Go through the gate and follow above the bank of the river through a sequence of fields until you come to a kissing gate. This leads you through a short section of wood to a further kissing gate after which a riverside path takes you along a field edge to Walmsley bridge (1.6 km).

Go left over the bridge and immediately turn right to cross a stile by a gate. Continue on the track directly ahead as it rises slightly to enable you to cross a further stile and gate. The path is now

Walmsley Bridge over the River Brock

Near Lower House

between two boundaries, the hedge on the right with a large amount of holly. After a further gate and stile follow the right-hand boundary down to another gate (currently missing) and stile which admits you to a large field. Follow the obvious path along and above the riverbank to the stile by a gate in the far right-hand corner of this field. Over this stile the grass is usually mowed and the field leads to a short enclosed path which soon leads you back to your start at New Bridge (1.5km).

WOODLANDS Many of the walks in this book rely on woodlands for adding variety to the landscape, however, Lancashire has a low percentage of cover. In the Fylde area the flat landscape looks well wooded due to the number of hedgerow trees that are seen. Many of these are old, however, and are not being replaced. In the Bowland foothills there is a mixture of woodlands. Some are maintained for pheasant rearing or form part of a rough shoot. Other rectangular block woodlands of conifers look strangely placed in a rounded landscape. The more deciduous woodlands, for example along the Brock, look at their best in autumn but many are poorly managed, if at all, and are slowly losing their native character

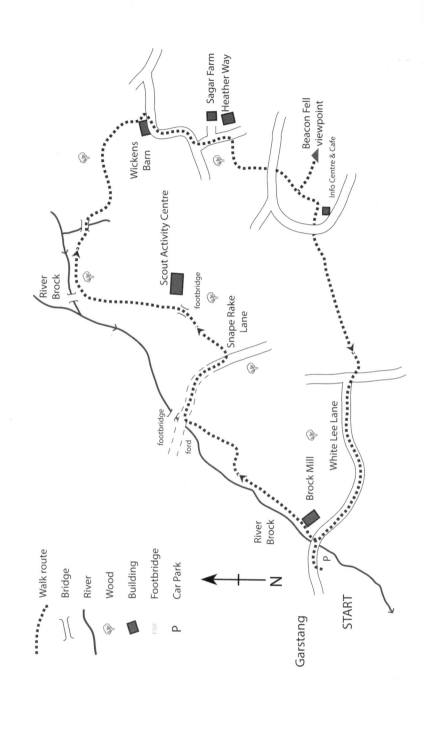

Walk route

Bridge

River

Wood

Building

Footbridge

P   Car Park

N

Garstang

START

River Brock

Brock Mill

White Lee Lane

footbridge

ford

footbridge

Snape Rake Lane

River Brock

Scout Activity Centre

Wickens Barn

Sagar Farm

Heather Way

Beacon Fell viewpoint

Info Centre & Cafe

The badger's river

BROCK BOTTOMS–BEACON FELL–BROCK BOTTOMS

DISTANCE: 8 kilometres (5 miles)

START: Brock Bottoms picnic site (SD 548431) or on Beacon Fell (SD 564426)

BUS: None

PARKING: Parking at the Brock Bottoms Picnic Site (SD 548431, PR3 0PP) or start on Beacon Fell (SD 564426) where there are pay and display car parks

MAP: O.S. Explorer OL41 The Forest of Bowland & Ribblesdale

TIP: Great walk, especially on a clear spring or autumn day. Certain parts of the route do become very busy at weekends and bank holidays. Some excellent woodlands and great viewpoints make this one of our favourite walks. With your O.S. map many additions can be made to the route

Leave the entrance to the car park and go right, over the bridge, and then immediately turn left to pass through the gap stile by the gateway. Keep left below Brock Mill house and the cottages and then climb the stile by the gate. Go into the field and follow the distinct path as it bends right and then goes ahead to pick up the left-hand fence by the River Brock. Follow this fence along and cross the stile in the far left-hand corner of the field. The path now continues between the river and the right-hand

Bleasedale and Fairsnape

fence until, at the far end of the field to your right, the path and right-hand fence bend away from the river, where you climb up through a narrow wood and up the short bluff beyond to reach a track. Go left down the track and just before the gate above the former cottage, with the Thirlmere aqueduct to your left, leave the track to the right along the garden wall to enter a wood. The path now follows at the bottom of the wood, with a field to your left, to eventually emerge on the riverbank. Follow this along to meet the footbridge and ford over the Brock and where Snape Rake Lane crosses the river (1.3km).

The woodlands you pass through show some of the natural woodland types of this area. Oak, elm, rowan, field maple, birch, ash, hazel and holly are the native trees but introduced sycamore and beech are changing the true character. Some of the ground vegetation of ferns and flowers suggest that this woodland is ancient in origin and, due to the steep valley sides, has never been fully cleared. Had it been felled then the erosion of the banks would be unthinkable.

River Brock

Go right and up the sunken hollow of Snape Rake Lane. There are some paths off to the right which appear tempting but beware: this is Boggy Wood and is true to its name! Continue along the lane when it becomes tarred, cross its highest point and, as it bends to the right, the wood on your left gives way to a field, and this is where you turn left through two stone gate posts and then a wooden gate. Follow the track down through the wood and, as it bends back sharp left, continue straight ahead to cross a footbridge, partially hidden, some 25 metres ahead. Over the bridge the path climbs to a sign telling you are entering Waddecar Scout Activity Centre. From here bear right to contour the short hillside to a campfire site and down the obvious path ahead. This leads to a track which you follow directly ahead, to pass a toilet block and continue on the track through the remainder of the campsite and wood to cross a double stile just after the track ends (1.3km).

Cross the field parallel to the right-hand wood and continue, through the gateway, into the next field and head directly towards a footbridge at the confluence of the two infant Brock rivers. Do not cross but turn right in front of the bridge to find a stile just beyond the ruins of Gill Barn. Back into woodland follow above the river by the left-hand fence and this leads,

Snape Rake Lane

eventually, to a footbridge over a tributary stream. Once over the bridge the distinct path climbs above the stream and, via a stile at the top, you enter a field (1 km).

From here the vista suddenly opens up with great views of Parlick, Fairsnape and the other fells encompassing Bleasdale, but also with Beacon Fell on your right. Fairsnape, at a height of just over 520m is one of the highest peaks of the Forest of Bowland.

Head just to the left of the rounded fell of Parlick to cross a field to a stile and gate in the fence across your away. Cross over this stile and then follow near the left-hand fence for the length of the next field. In the far left-hand field corner pass through the gate directly facing you and the subsequent gate. Turn right in this next field, follow the right-hand fence and then cross the stile in the far right-hand field corner. This admits you to an enclosed path which goes left and then bends right to a further stile and the metalled road (900 metres).

Go right on the road, round the left-hand bend, along a straight stretch (with Beacon Fell directly ahead) and then round the right-hand corner. Just after this corner a track goes off left which you take. Keep ahead when this track forks and shortly afterwards, almost opposite a house, a well-signed stile on your right readmits you back into a field. Follow near the left-hand boundary (at the time of writing becoming increasingly

Fairsnape and Parlick

derelict) and after around 100m a signed and well waymarked path enables you to turn left and follow the path up to a stile and, just after, the circular road around Beacon Fell. Cross the road diagonally right and take the gated forest track, through depressing conifer woodlands, up towards the shoulder of the open fell. Ignore any paths which cross your way but when you reach the next woodland section (currently by a fence corner) you can make the short ascent (to your left) to the highest point of the fell (1 km).

Beacon Fell was an historic beacon site (see the visitor centre for more information) and the view from the top is magnificent, from the Bowland Fells to Pendle Hill, around to the Forest of Rossendale and then the Welsh Clwydian hills and the Lancashire coast. The summit of Black Combe is the most prominent Lake District fell.

From this point continue straight ahead, go straight across a footpath junction and then descend to the car park, visitor centre, toilets and café (400 m).

Sculpture on Beacon Fell

Leave the visitor centre by the café entrance and take the path with stone setts to your left as it climbs past the sculpture of a head (much loved by young children!) as it continues to bend left, pass above the visitor centre, and eventually down to the road by a further car park. Go straight across the road and descend to a gate through which a distinct path leads you down by a series of gates through memorial plantings and open ground to eventually reach a footbridge. Over the footbridge cross this last field towards the most prominent overhead wire pole and gain the metalled road by a stile. Go right on the road but, almost immediately, turn left down White Lee Lane to return to your starting point at the picnic site (2.1 km).

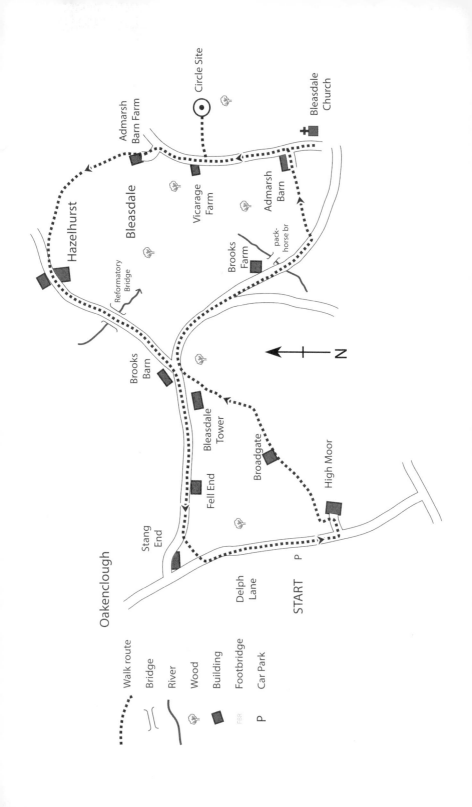

Fellside parish: exploring Bleasdale

OAKENCLOUGH–BLEASDALE TOWER–OAKENCLOUGH

DISTANCE: 9.1 km (5.5 miles)

START: Delph Lane, south of Oakenclough (SD 546455)

BUS: There is no public transport available

PARKING: There are spaces just off the road on Delph Lane, south of Oakenclough at (SD 546455, PR3 1UN)

MAP : *O.S. Explorer OL41 The Forest of Bowland & Ribblesdale*

TIP: Bleasdale is a gem of a dale but the lack of public roads makes parking for a shorter walk most difficult. If you want a longer walk then start on Beacon Fell. Great in all seasons but obviously a sunny day is preferable. One intriguing prehistoric site is visited. Some tracks and private roads but a few wet fields to cross as well!

From the car parking area turn right down the road until a concrete road goes left to High Moor. Follow this track until just before the house and yard you can enter the field on the left by a gate. In the field follow the right-hand boundary around to a kissing gate, behind the house, and then cross the next, short field to pass through another, obvious kissing gate. Go down the next long field by the right-hand fence with Broadgate Farm off to your left. Go through the gate facing you at the bottom of the field, go ahead on the track and, at the junction, cross slightly to your right to pass between two stone gate posts (900 m).

In the field go along the left-hand hedge and, just after it bends, go through the gate in the field corner to your left. This gives access to a farm track which you follow to the right, past a barn and it eventually goes right, through a gate into a field. Just before this gate you continue on an obvious route between two narrow woods and re-enter a field by a further gate. Go half-left up the field and leave it by a kissing gate by a gate in the far corner of the field. In the next field, with Bleasdale Tower on your left, go along the right-hand fence, through another gate, follow a short track to a further gate and this gives access to a metalled road (1km).

Bleasdale Tower was built as a shooting lodge when the owners lived at Quernmore Park.

Go right down the metalled road at the junction facing you, keep left at the next junction and descend to the bridge by Brooks Farm over the River Brock. Look left to see the packhorse bridge at Brooks Farm which is probably from the mid-nineteenth century when it replaced a ford. The bridge would be on a route, no longer public, for taking wool to Pennine manufacturing

Below Parlick

Meadow pipit

Redshank

areas. The route probably started at Coolam (see later). Continue up the metalled road and when it bends right by a wood go left along a track between a hedge and the small wood to a gate. Through the gate go up the field towards a copse and Parlick Pike and when past the copse go to the gate by the right-hand side of Admarsh Barn. Leave the yard by a further gate to join another track (1.4km).

The house was originally a barn and has a 1720 date stone. If you go just to the right over the cattle-grid you come directly to St Eadmer's Church at Admarsh in Bleasdale, a nineteenth-century church building with a 'quaint' Last Supper over the altar and two odd faces peering from carvings on old chairs. It is the only known dedication to St Eadmer, possibly the monk Eadbert who carried on St Cuthbert's work at Lindisfarne and was buried in the saint's tomb. The church claims there has been a place of worship on this site since at least 1577. Windows, perhaps from an earlier Elizabethan structure, can be found in the church tower. If you use the toilet at the church, please leave a donation.

Emerging from Admarsh Barn turn left down the track to reach Vicarage Farm (500m). Over the cattle-grid and opposite the driveway to the house, on your right you will see a gate and a sign to Bleasdale Circle. To reach the circle site go through the gate, go up the field by the left-hand fence, pass through a kissing gate in the top left-hand field corner, and then cross to a further kissing gate in the clump of trees that hide the circle site. Return by this route to the estate road (600 metres).

The circle site, rediscovered in 1899, is marked now by unsightly concrete stumps where once eleven wooden posts stood. In the central area was a small barrow whose excavation yielded graves with two cremations in collared urns and an incense cup. A ditch

*and a timber palisade, some 46
m in diameter, surrounded the
circle. This woodhenge site has
been dated at various times
but the on-site information
suggests around 1700 BC i.e.
Early Bronze Age. The entrance
to the circle points towards
the Fairsnape ridge where lies
the man-made gouge into the
ridge called 'Nicks Chair'. Was it a contemporary alignment with the
circle? If so, does it give the circle a calendar function? A similar site
has been found nearer Chipping.*

Bleasdale Circle

Continue along the estate road from Vicarage Farm until you
pass over a cattle-grid at the entrance to Admarsh Barn Farm.
Over this immediately turn right to follow the right-hand fence
along, pass the rear of a barn and enter a field. In the field follow
the right-hand fence, cross a stile by gate in the field corner,
continue along by the right-hand fence and then cross, in short
succession a bridge and gate. Again follow along the right-hand
fence to descend to a ford where you cross two footbridges and
the subsequent stile by a gate (800 metres). This is the infant
River Brock of a very different character from that seen in our
earlier walks.

Continue along by the right-hand boundary but, on passing
under overhead power lines, bear half right and cross the field to
a stile which lies in the middle of the boundary across your way.
Climb the next field half-left to reach an access track just before
Hazelhurst. Go left on the track past Hazelhurst Cottage and the
extensive farm buildings (500 metres).

*Hazelhurst and the adjacent Coolam (a ruined house whose
character was totally eradicated in a restoration) were once part
of a wool-producing hamlet of six cottages inhabited by some
70 people. Most of these were involved in wool spinning and*

handloom weaving prior to the goods being sent by packhorse to the wool towns of East Lancashire and Yorkshire. The remains of stocks can be noted on your right just after the cottage. It feels that our path from the church to here could also have been a packhorse route from Coolam.

Continue along the access road until you come to a T-junction at Brooks Barn (1.3km).

Along the way we descend, in the wood, to a bridge which has a date plaque (1858–9) on one face (now hard to discern any text) and a mason's stone on the left parapet. The bridge was built by the boys from the reformatory. It is worth looking over the bridge to see the enormity of the structure. Later, on the left, before we arrive at Brooks Barn, are the buildings (built 1857) which once held a reformatory school for boys from urban backgrounds, who were extensively used as 'inexpensive' farm and estate workers. They were used, for example, to turn the fields by hand prior to planting crops or for reclaiming moorland. Some 130 street children, from places like Liverpool, were moved here for what today we may regard as slave labour but in Victorian times it was held up as a model institution.

Turn right at the junction, go up the metalled estate road, passing Bleasdale Tower, the gate house and eventually reaching a gate by Fell End Farm. Continue through this gate along the road and when the open field on the right narrows and you can see the white cottage and gate at Stang End, leave the road by going left near a small concrete post, go down through a small gate, along through the narrow wood to the road. Your start is down the road to the left (2.7 km). With an O.S. map a slightly longer footpath route can be found to return to your starting point.

VEGETATION can appear quickly, especially during the summer; nettles and brambles seem to love to grow near stiles and footbridges. A good tip would be to carry a pair of secateurs just in case the hard-pressed councils have been unable to clear the growth

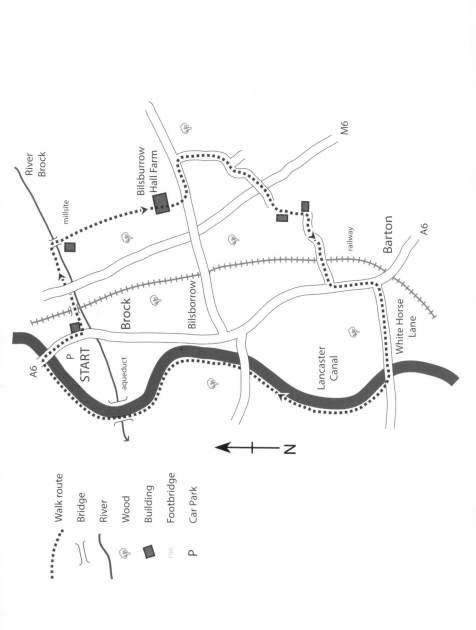

Exploring Bilsborrow and Brock

BARTON GRANGE–BILSBORROW–BARTON GRANGE

DISTANCE: 8.4 km (5.3 miles)

START: A6 road by Barton Grange Garden Centre (SD 511406)

PARKING: Barton Grange is a private business but cars may be parked here if you do the walk and use the café or other interests of the site which include a garden centre, curling rink and cinema. If not, please park politely in Bilsborrow near the church and commence the walk from there (PR3 0BT)

BUS: The Preston to Lancaster Bus service number 40 to Brock (Barton Grange Garden Centre stop). The walk is described from here

MAP: O.S. Explorer 286 Blackpool and Preston

TIP: A walk for any season but best to avoid weekends and bank holidays. A crisp winter day would be ideal although it would exclude some potential wildlife sightings. A relatively flat walk that makes use of some of the quietest parts of the canal towpath and some unusual sections of footpath. Please respect the parking arrangements at Barton Grange

From the bus stop on the A6 go to the garage forecourt (cross the road if you have come from the Preston direction) and walk through display area to ascend the huge green footbridge over the main-line railway. Descend to a 'garden' and then follow the obvious track as it bends to reach the riverbank and goes under the M6. Follow this track until an aluminium footbridge allows you to cross the River Brock at Matshead (800 metres).

The garden marks the site of the former Brock railway station which for many ramblers in the early and mid-twentieth century was their main access to the various walks along the River Brock. The river here is much quieter and more confined than in the upper stages of our other walks.

Over the footbridge go straight ahead through the garden gates of Millwood House and walk directly towards the left-hand side of their garage. Go past the garage and continue ahead until you are opposite the end of the white houses. Here you go left through a garden gate, under a bough of shrubs and then turn left on a short enclosed path found to the immediate left of a gate marked private (100 metres).

Barton Grange Marina

On entering the first garden glance left to see the remains of the water wheel that was once the power for this former paper mill.

At the end of this path climb the stile to enter a small field which is crossed directly to a further stile. Follow the right-hand hedge in the next, larger field to pass through a double steel gate in the far right-hand field corner. Immediately go through the adjacent similar gate on your left and again go along the right-hand boundary to a footbridge which gives access to a farm track. Follow this farm track all the way along to Bilsborrow Hall Farm. On entering the farmyard walk straight through the middle of the huge barn facing you, with cattle stalls at either side, emerge into a further part of the yard and go slightly left to find the farm access track which, via a gate, leads you to the metalled Bilsborrow Lane (1.1 km).

There are few footpaths which bring you into such close proximity to farm life!

Walkers from Bilsborrow should join the walk here.

Turn left on the road, cross over, and take the first lane off right to Fishers Farm and the equestrian centre. The metalled lane takes you towards a huge barn where you ignore the left turn to Fishers and continue around the barn, over the M6 and down towards Mount Pleasant Farm where the equestrian establishment is situated. Go left immediately in front of the farm house and follow the enclosed bridle path as it goes down into a hollow and then continues for some distance until it emerges on a metalled lane. The lane could be quite old, as with similar lanes such as Snape Rake and at Brock Bottoms. They appear to have been so worn down through the surrounding ground, perhaps by packhorses, they could be described as 'hollow ways'. Follow the metalled lane to the right and it eventually crosses the railway to emerge on the A6 (1.8 km).

Turn left along the A6, cross when safe, and continue until just past the restaurant, and when opposite the garage you can turn right down White Horse Lane. This metalled cul-de-sac is followed all the way to White Horse Bridge over the canal (1.1 km).

Go down the steps to the towpath, turn left and follow the canal all the way to bridge 47 which is on the A6 just above your starting point. You can leave the canal on either side of the road bridge (3.5 km).

On your return journey views of the Bowland fells often form tantalising backdrops. If you joined the walk at Bilsborrow you can shorten the walk and leave the canal at bridge 45. Note the traditional elliptical-shaped arch of the original Rennie bridges over the canal, and do spend a few moments looking at the Rennie aqueduct which carries the canal over the river Brock just before the end of your walk.

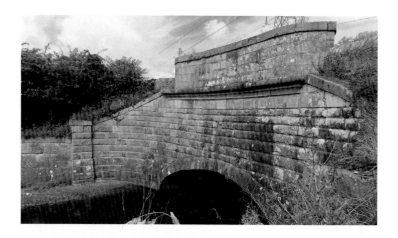

Brock aqueduct and information plaque